THE BREAD MACHINE COOKBOOK VI
HAND-SHAPED BREADS FROM THE DOUGH CYCLE
Donna Rathmell German

BRISTOL PUBLISHING ENTERPRISES
San Leandro, California

A Nitty Gritty® Cookbook

©1995 Bristol Publishing Enterprises, Inc.,
P.O. Box 1737, San Leandro, California 94577.

Printed in the United States of America.

ISBN 1-55867-121-8

Cover design: Frank Paredes
Cover photography: John Benson
Food stylist: Suzanne Carreiro
Illustrator: James Balkovek

CONTENTS

THE DOUGH CYCLE 1

MAKING, SHAPING AND EMBELLISHING DOUGH 2

    BREAD MACHINE DOUGH CYCLE: GENERAL DIRECTIONS 2

    PREPARING DOUGH TO BAKE LATER 4

    SHAPING DOUGH 5

    CRUST TREATMENTS 13

INGREDIENTS 16

    NUTRITIONAL ANALYSIS 17

ROLLS, BAGUETTES AND BREADSTICKS . . . 18

SWEET ROLLS AND COFFEE CAKES 51

BAGELS, ENGLISH MUFFINS AND DOUGHNUTS . 86

ETHNIC BREADS 105

HOLIDAY BREADS 138

FINISHING TOUCHES 156

SOURCES 165

BIBLIOGRAPHY 166

INDEX 167

Many thanks to Joyce Arroyo, who was invaluable in testing recipes,
and to Chlorie Denmark, whose help kept me sane!

As always, my husband and daughters stood by my side
and never complained about bread machines starting
in the very early hours of the morning and going all day long.

Thanks to all the friends, neighbors, teachers,
Navy sailors and homeless shelter residents
who ate the thousands of rolls and loaves of bread.

Special thanks to the following people for recipes:
Carol Neel, *Olive Walnut Bread*
Karen Hubachek, *Double Chocolate Rolls*
Mr. and Mrs. Buck Neal Polk, *Bolillos and Teleras*
Raymond G. Johnson, *Pan Dulce*
Donna Harrington, *Tadale*

THE DOUGH CYCLE

Using the dough cycle on your bread machine gives you the opportunity to be as creative as you wish, and allows you to use almost any bread recipe in your bread machine to produce hand-shaped bread or bread baked in a container in your regular oven.

The great joy of using a bread machine's dough cycle is that you do not struggle with the first kneading of the dough, which is the most difficult (and messy!). Once the machine has kneaded the dough and allowed it to rise, it is ready for you to shape according to tradition or to what suits your mood. Whether making rolls or a loaf, there are hundreds of variations of shapes. This book is a compilation of traditional breads, ethnic breads and some new variations on older themes. All recipes are made using the dough cycle of your bread machine.

Any yeast-raised bread recipe that contains approximately 4 cups of flour or less may be made using the dough cycle of your machine. Use your favorite family recipe for traditionally made bread, or any of the recipes in my previous books. Add the ingredients to your machine in the manner suggested by your manufacturer and let the machine take the dough through the first rising. If a soft dough is being used, you will need to use a pan to hold the shape. Firm doughs may be baked in pans or formed into round or oblong loaves, rolls or other shapes.

It may be necessary to adjust baking time and temperature, depending on the recipe and form of the dough. In general, breads with high sugar and/or fat content should be baked at 350°F or lower. Recipes for breads with crisp, crusty exteriors should be baked at higher temperatures, from 400° to as much as 500°. Small rolls will take less time than large forms.

MAKING, SHAPING AND EMBELLISHING DOUGH

BREAD MACHINE DOUGH CYCLE: GENERAL DIRECTIONS

The dough cycle kneads the dough and lets it rise once, for a long period. Upon completion of the cycle, the dough is removed from the machine, shaped by hand, generally allowed to rise again and baked in a conventional oven.

All machines, even a 1 lb. machine, are capable of kneading up to 4 cups of flour. *Please do not try to bake these recipes in your machine*. If you have a 1 lb. machine and the dough is rising too high, you may either deflate the dough (by puncturing it) and allow it to continue with the cycle, or you may remove the dough and proceed to shape it, as it is probably only a few minutes from completion of the cycle.

Many machines have a double kneading on the dough cycle with a short rest of 5 to 10 minutes in between. The dough is then left to rise in the warm machine for 30 minutes to 1 hour. When testing recipes, I allow the machine to complete the entire cycle. In some cases, however, when making something for my family or when I am not testing, I have been known to shorten the dough cycle. For example, if your dough cycle takes 1½ hours, you probably have a kneading period of about 15 minutes, a short rest and then about 10 more minutes of kneading before about 1 hour of rising. If you are really in a time crunch, it is possible to allow the machine to knead the first time (for the 10 or 15 minutes) and then, during the rest period, turn off the machine and let the dough sit for 45 to 60 minutes. I emphasize that I tested these recipes using the complete dough cycle. I have, however, received enough phone calls and letters asking about shortening the cycle that, yes, I acknowledge you can experiment.

If you own a DAK, Welbilt 100 or Citizen machine, allow the manual cycle to knead once, and the dough to rise for about 1 hour. Then turn off the machine and remove the dough before it goes into the second full kneading. If you allow the machine to knead a full cycle after a 1-hour rising, the dough often becomes so airy and light that it is difficult to work with.

While most bread machines have timer features on the regular bake cycle, very few have a dough cycle which works on a timer. If you want to make a dough for a specific time, you can figure out the math for your machine and set it on the regular timer. The concern when doing this is that you must be home in time to stop the machine so that it does not go into a bake cycle — this is extremely important if you are using a dough recipe with a higher amount of flour than your machine calls for. Also, remember not to use any recipe with eggs, milk or cheese (which could spoil) on the timer.

Some machines have a stir-down feature which rotates the kneading paddle for 20 to 30 seconds just before the buzzer sounds to indicate that the dough cycle is complete. The purpose of this is to allow air in the dough to escape. A traditional bread recipe often indicates that you should punch down the dough or knead it a second time. When using the machine's dough cycle, merely taking the dough out of the machine punches it down and it is not necessary for you to do so.

You may find it helpful to place the dough on a lightly floured work surface and to dust it with a little flour to prevent it from sticking (to your hands or to the work surface). You should take care not to add too much flour as it can make the final product hard and tough. Some recipes such as brioche or challah are naturally sticky and you may be tempted to add flour to work with it. In this case, it is better to grease your hands and the work surface instead of using flour. I simply spray the work surface and my hands with a nonstick vegetable spray.

When dividing dough into a given number of equal sizes, roll the dough into a log. Divide the log in half and then divide each half in half (quarters). Divide each quarter into the appropriate number necessary.

If at any time during the rolling or shaping the dough becomes difficult to work, let it rest for 5 to 10 minutes to relax. It will then be easier to shape.

Spray all pans with a nonstick vegetable spray, or grease them with butter.

PREPARING DOUGH TO BAKE LATER

Refrigerating dough: Dough may be made, shaped, placed on a greased baking sheet and completely, but loosely, covered with plastic wrap. Place it in the refrigerator for 2 to 10 hours. When ready to bake, remove the dough from the refrigerator to a warm, draft-free location to bring it to room temperature while you preheat the oven. Bake according to directions in the recipe. The dough will rise in the refrigerator, but the cold temperature makes the dough rise more slowly.

Freezing dough: Dough may be made, shaped, placed on a greased baking sheet, covered with plastic wrap and then placed in the freezer until firm. At that point, it may be placed in a plastic bag and frozen for up to 2 weeks. When ready to bake, remove dough from the freezer and place on a greased baking sheet in a warm, draft-free location to thaw and rise for about 4 hours. Bake according to directions.

SHAPING DOUGH

Each recipe in this book includes directions for a simple shape, but this section will give you ideas to try with any recipe as you desire. You should watch the baking times when experimenting with different shapes. Larger rolls may take longer to bake and vice versa.

Crescent rolls: Roll the dough into 1 or 2 large rounds on a lightly floured work surface. A 4-cup recipe will easily make 2 rounds. A 3-cup recipe will make a large round and very large crescents, or 2 rounds and smaller crescents. Using a knife or pizza wheel, cut each round into 8 equal pieces (as you would a pie). Roll each piece firmly from the wide end to the narrow end. Place the pointed side down on a greased baking sheet and bend the outer ends down to form a curve. Cover, let rise and bake according to directions.

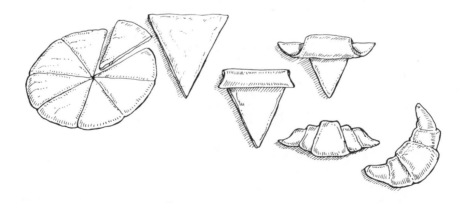

Flower (knot) rolls: Divide the dough into 8 to 12 equal pieces. Roll each piece into an 8- to 10-inch rope, about ½ inch in diameter. Tie into a loose knot with long ends. Bring one end over and under the roll and the other end up and over, and tuck it into the center of the knot. Cover, let rise and bake according to directions.

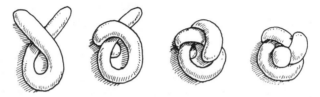

Coil rolls: Divide the dough into 8 to 12 equal pieces. Roll each piece into an 8- to 10-inch rope, about ½ inch in diameter. Coil the rope around on itself and tuck the end underneath. Cover, let rise and bake according to directions.

Cloverleaf rolls: Divide the dough into 36 equal pieces (about 1 inch in size). Dip each piece in melted butter and place 3 in each lightly greased muffin cup. Cover, let rise and bake according to directions.

Parker House rolls: Roll the dough on a lightly floured work surface into a large, ¼-inch-thick rectangle. Using a 2½- to 3-inch biscuit cutter (or similar tool), cut into rounds. Brush each round with melted butter and then fold each round almost in half (with the buttered side in), pressing on the fold. Cover, let rise and bake according to directions.

Fan rolls: Roll the dough into a large, thin rectangle. Using your fingers or a pastry brush, brush the top of the rectangle with about 1 tbs. melted butter. With a sharp knife, pastry or pizza wheel, cut the dough into small rectangles (about 1½ x 2 inches). Place 5 rectangles on top of each other and place short side down in a greased muffin cup. As the dough rises and bakes, the rolls will fan out. Cover, let rise and bake according to directions.

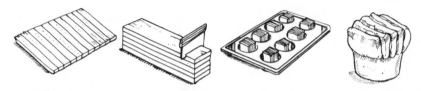

Twisted breadsticks: Form the dough into 20 or 24 equal balls. Roll each ball to form a rope 8 to 10 inches long. Starting with the first rope made (this rest allows the dough to relax and makes it easier to work with), take one end in one hand and hold it in place as you twist with the other hand. Either leave the dough in a long rope or pinch the ends together to make a twisted ring. Cover, let rise and bake according to directions.

Jelly-roll (and slices): Roll the dough into a large, thin rectangle. If a filling is to be used, the filling should be spread evenly over the rectangle, leaving a ½-inch border around the edge. Starting with the wide edge closest to you, roll the dough tightly, encasing the filling. Pinch to seal. For rolls, slice into about 12 equal slices. Cover, let rise and bake according to directions.

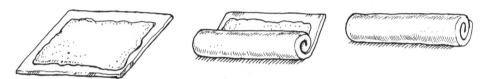

Kaiser rolls: Divide dough into 8 to 10 equal pieces and roll each piece into a 6- or 7-inch round. Fold one edge toward the middle. Starting about halfway along that fold, fold another piece toward the middle. Continue around the edge until you have 5 folds. Tuck the last half of the last fold under the first fold and press firmly to seal. Place folded side up on a greased baking sheet. Cover, let rise and bake according to directions.

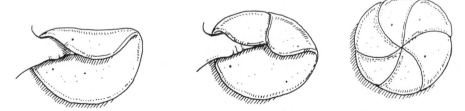

Braid: Divide the dough into 3 equal pieces and roll each piece into a long rope. The three strands should be braided together as you would hair. If you have difficulty starting the braid, begin in the center and work toward the ends. Seal and tuck the ends underneath and place the braid on a greased baking sheet. Cover, let rise and bake according to directions.

Mock braid: Roll the dough into a large rectangle. Using scissors, a sharp knife, pastry or pizza wheel, cut 1-inch strips down each side, from the center third to the edge. Fold strips over the center, alternating side, and angling each folded strip toward you. Tuck the ends inside to give the appearance of a braid. Place on a greased baking sheet. Cover, let rise and bake according to directions.

Filled rolls: Form the dough into equal balls a little bigger than an egg. Flatten each ball into a thick round and place the filling in the middle. Pull the edges of the dough over the filling and press tightly together to seal the filling inside. Place seam side down in greased muffin cups, or on a baking sheet. Cover, let rise and bake according to directions.

Pretzels: Form the dough into 10 equal balls. Roll each ball into a long rope, about 15 to 20 inches long, and shape into a wide U. Cross one end over the other and press together gently. Pick up the ends that are crossed and cross a second time. Fold the twisted portion over the bottom of the U following the illustration. Cover, let rise and bake according to directions.

Daisy wheel: Divide the dough into 9 equal pieces. Roll one piece into a ball and place it in the center of a greased pizza pan or round baking sheet. Shape remaining 8 pieces into long ovals and place them around the center ball, radiating out from the center like petals. Cover, let rise and bake according to directions. After baking, remove in one piece to cool on a wire rack.

Cookie cutter wreaths: One of my favorite (and so very easy) gifts is a bread wreath. Over the years, I have made orange pumpkin wreaths for Halloween, green tree wreaths for Christmas, red heart wreaths for Valentine's Day, or other shaped wreaths for any time of the year.

Add a few drops of appropriate food coloring to the liquid. Roll the dough into a large, 1/2-inch-thick rectangle on a lightly floured surface. Using a 2 1/2- to 3-inch cookie cutter (pumpkin, heart, star, etc.), cut the dough into as many rolls as possible. Place each roll on the outer rim of a lightly greased (disposable if you're giving them away) pizza pan so that the rolls touch each other slightly. If you have rolls left, place 2 or 3 in the center or use another pan. Cover, let rise and bake according to directions.

CRUST TREATMENTS

Washes: A wash is brushed on the bread dough just before it goes into the oven. Use a pastry brush (or your fingers) to gently "paint" the top of the dough — be careful not to push down and deflate the risen dough.

- An egg white beaten with 1 tbs. water will give the bread a shiny, crisp crust. Milk may be used instead of water for a softer but still shiny crust.
- A complete egg or just the yolk mixed with 1 to 2 tbs. milk or water is used for a shiny, richer and darker-colored crust.
- Milk or cream (alone) gives a shiny finish (not quite as dark as an egg) to the bread.
- Any kind of oil or melted butter may be brushed on to give the bread a soft crust.
- A honey wash gives bread a sweet, glossy finish. Use 1 to 2 tbs. each honey and water.
- Cold water may be brushed or sprayed (use a plant mister or similar device) on the bread for a crisp, chewy crust for French or Italian breads.
- Lemon juice mixed with 2 to 3 tbs. sugar gives a fruity, sweet flavor.

Embellishments: Seeds, herbs, nuts and similar toppings are added to the tops of breads after the dough has been lightly washed, just before it is baked. The wash acts as "glue."

- Seeds such as poppy, sesame, fennel, anise, caraway, celery, or sunflower add flavor to breads and give them a professional-looking finish.
- Similar in size to seeds, small grains such as teff or amaranth can also be used.

- Rolled grains such as oats or wheat add an interesting appearance and texture.
- Herbs may be sprinkled on top of bread which has been washed with water or oil.
- Finely chopped nuts may be used either before baking with a wash or after baking on top of a glaze.

"Crusty" Crusts: Baguettes and many other breads require a crispy, crunchy crust which is aided by adding steam to the baking process. This may be done in one of several ways or in combination.

- Use a clean mister (such as a plant mister) to spray the dough just before you put it in the oven and then mist it again two more times during the first half of the baking. Simply open the oven door and briefly spray the mist into the oven, but be careful not to spray any electrical elements.
- Use a pastry brush and brush the bread with COLD water just before you put the bread into the oven.
- Place a shallow pan of an inch or so of water on the bottom shelf or bottom of the preheated oven about 5 minutes before putting the bread in the oven.
- Place a shallow, empty pan on the bottom shelf or bottom of the oven when you start to preheat it. Just before you place the dough in the oven, put 4 or 5 ice cubes into the empty, hot pan. Be very careful not to spill the ice on an electrical element!
- Clay baking tiles (or pizza or baking stones) give breads an extra crispy crust. If you

preheat tiles or a stone in the oven (for the best crust), the dough should be placed on a cornmeal-covered pizza peel or a rimless baking sheet to rise so that it may be easily slipped directly onto the stone. The dough may also be placed on parchment paper and the dough and paper together placed directly on the stone.

- Clay ovens (la cloche) have both a top and a bottom. The top may be turned upside down and placed in a large pan in the sink and filled with water to soak while the dough is rising and the oven is preheating. The clay bottom could be preheated (place the dough on parchment paper so that you can get it into the bottom easily) or the dough may be placed in the clay bottom to rise. Once the dough is ready to put in the oven, empty the water from the top and place it on top of the clay bottom. It may take a little longer to bake this way; I remove the lid during the last minute or two.

- A perforated pizza pan is perfect for crisp, crusty breads or breadsticks.

- I tested several different types of baguette pans for this book and prefer a perforated baguette pan, much like the pizza pans. Spray it with a nonstick vegetable spray such as PAM. If you do not have a baguette pan, use a perforated pizza pan or a plain baking sheet. These pans generally hold 2 or 3 baguettes.

- Cast-iron breadstick pans make wonderful, thick breadsticks, or as my girls call them, mini-baguettes. Cast-iron corn stick pans in the shape of corn, cactus, etc., may also be used for breadsticks. If you do not have one, use a perforated pizza pan or a plain baking sheet.

INGREDIENTS

All-purpose flour is a combination of a flour milled from a soft, low-protein wheat (used for cakes and pastries) and a hard, high-protein bread flour. I generally use all-purpose flour when I want a softer, more tender crumb to the bread.

Bread flour is milled from hard wheat, which is very high in protein and gluten. Bread flour is used in all recipes that are baked in the bread machines, as the resulting loaves are higher rising and have a better texture. Because you control the length of rising time with recipes made by hand, I recommend using bread flour in recipes when you want a crisper crust and a heartier crumb.

Herbs that are fresh may be found in the produce section of most grocery stores and are preferred for flavor over the dried ones in bread baking. It is not essential to measure the herbs exactly, as it is largely a matter of taste. I generally pull off the leaves, tear them into small pieces and throw them straight into the machine pan.

Lemon and orange peel, dried, are found in the spice section of your grocery store. If you desire, however, it is quite easy to use fresh lemon or orange peel (zest). Any kitchen or specialty shop sells a "lemon zester" for a few dollars, which you use directly on the citrus fruit (much like grating cheese). I grate zest right over the bread machine pan and estimate what looks right. Generally, removing zest from an entire lemon will equate to ½ tsp. dried lemon peel — an entire orange equals about 1 tsp. dried orange peel. Whichever you prefer, adjust the quantity to your taste.

Milk can be whole, or reduced butterfat. To reduce fat, I use skim milk whenever milk is called for.

Yeast listed in these recipes is fast or quick yeast (also called bread machine yeast), and all testing was done with this type of yeast. If you are using the regular, active dry yeast, simply heap the amount given in the recipe.

NUTRITIONAL ANALYSIS

Recipes that are divided into a specific number of pieces are nutritionally analyzed per piece. Because the majority of recipes make 12 pieces (or a number easily divisible by 12), those recipes that are for 1 loaf are also given per $1/12$ amount for comparison. How many actual pieces or servings are obtained from 1 loaf of bread depends on how you slice it. Analyses were done using skim milk, unsalted butter, canola oil and large eggs when those ingredients are called for. If there are two ingredients listed, the first one is used in the analysis. Optional ingredients are not included, nor are glazes and frying fat. Fillings are included in the analysis unless otherwise indicated.

Calories are rounded to the nearest calorie; nutrients measured by grams are measured to the nearest 1 gram (if less than 0.5 grams, are listed as 0); nutrients measured by milligrams are measured to the nearest 1 milligram (if less than 1, are listed as 0).

ROLLS, BAGUETTES AND BREADSTICKS

PARKER HOUSE ROLLS . . . 19

BRIOCHE 20

HAWAIIAN PINEAPPLE ROLLS 22

CHEESE SCALLION BREAD . 23

HERB-FILLED LOAF 24

YOGURT CHEESE 25

POTATO RYE CHEESE ROLLS . 26

CHEESE-FILLED HERB ROLLS 28

HERB ROLLS 30

OLIVE WALNUT BREAD . . . 31

HERBED MONKEY BREAD . . 32

SIMPLE BAGUETTES 33

SPONGE BAGUETTES . . . 34

MEXICAN-FLAVORED
  BAGUETTES/BREADSTICKS 36

JALAPEÑO CHEESE CORNMEAL
  BAGUETTES/BREADSTICKS 38

ORANGE GINGER BAGUETTES/
  BREADSTICKS 40

TOMATO HERB BAGUETTES/
  BREADSTICKS 42

PARMESAN PEPPER
  BAGUETTES/BREADSTICKS 44

ITALIAN BREADSTICKS
  (GRISSINI) 46

PRETZELS 48

BEER BREADSTICKS 50

PARKER HOUSE ROLLS

Yield: about 12 rolls

*The Parker House in historic Boston made these uniquely shaped rolls famous. This basic dinner roll recipe may also be made in other shapes (see pages 5-12). Why not serve with a flavored butter from **Finishing Touches**, beginning on page 156?*

DOUGH

1¼ cups milk
2 tbs. butter or margarine
1 tbs. sugar

½ tsp. salt
3 cups all-purpose flour
1½ tsp. rapid or quick yeast

WASH

½-1 tbs. butter, melted

Remove dough from the machine upon completion of the dough cycle. Roll dough on a lightly floured work surface into a large, ¼-inch-thick rectangle. With a 2½- or 3-inch biscuit cutter (or similar tool), cut into rounds. Brush each round with melted butter and then fold each round almost in half (with buttered side in), pressing on the fold (see page 7). Place on a greased baking sheet or in muffin cups, cover and let rise for 30 to 45 minutes. Bake in a preheated 350° oven for 12 to 15 minutes.

*per ¹⁄₁₂ **recipe** 145 calories, 3 g fat (1 g sat fat), 4 g protein, 26 g carbohydrate, 6 mg cholesterol, 103 mg sodium*

BRIOCHE

Fill rich brioche dough with just a little cheese, meat or preserves for a special delicious treat (don't use too much or it will leak out). This recipe makes wonderful, rich rolls without filling. Just follow the directions and omit it. Start with 3 cups flour and add more if you need it to make the dough the right consistency.

BRIOCHE DOUGH

1/2 cup milk
1/4 cup butter
3 eggs
2 tbs. sugar

1 tsp. salt
3-3 1/4 cups all-purpose flour
2 tsp. rapid or quick yeast

FILLING

4-5 oz. Brie cheese, cut into 1-inch cubes,
  or your favorite preserve, marmalade or apple butter, about 1 tsp. per roll,
  or your favorite filling, about 1 tsp. per roll

WASH

1 egg beaten with 1-2 tbs. milk or cream

Remove dough from the machine upon completion of the dough cycle. If dough is sticky, grease your hands and the work surface, or knead in only enough flour so that it is easily handled, and divide into 12 equal pieces. Form each piece into a ball and stuff each one with about a 1-inch cheese cube or 1 tsp. filling (see page 11). Pinch ends together to seal. Place rolls in greased muffin cups. Cover and let rise in a warm, draft-free location for about 30 minutes. Brush with egg wash. Bake in a preheated 350° oven for about 15 to 20 minutes.

per ¹⁄₁₂ **recipe without filling** *179 calories, 5 g fat (3 g sat fat), 5 g protein, 27 g carbohydrate, 64 mg cholesterol, 200 mg sodium*

HAWAIIAN PINEAPPLE ROLLS

While one would assume that these are delicious as breakfast rolls (and they are), they also make fabulous ham sandwiches! Use your favorite shaping technique on pages 5-12. If you are serving these as sweet buns, glaze them while warm.

1⅛ cups pineapple juice
2 tbs. butter
1 tsp. grated ginger root, or to taste, or ¼ tsp. ground ginger
2 tbs. brown sugar
½ tsp. salt
3 cups all-purpose flour
2 tsp. rapid or quick yeast

Remove dough from the machine upon completion of the dough cycle and place on a lightly floured work surface. Form dough into 8 to 10 balls and place on a lightly greased baking sheet. Cover with a kitchen towel and let rise for about 1 hour in a warm, draft-free location. Bake in a preheated 350° oven for 15 to 20 minutes.

per ⅒ **recipe** *183 calories, 3 g fat (2 g sat fat), 4 g protein, 36 g carbohydrate, 6 mg cholesterol, 109 mg sodium*

CHEESE SCALLION BREAD

Yield: 2 loaves

The combination of fresh green onions and sharp cheddar cheese rolled into this bread makes it an all-time winner.

DOUGH

1⅛ cups milk
2 tbs. butter or margarine
1 tbs. sugar

½ tsp. salt
3 cups all-purpose flour
1½ tsp. rapid or quick yeast

FILLING

1 cup grated sharp cheddar cheese
2-4 green onions, diced

Remove dough from the machine upon completion of the dough cycle and divide in half. On a lightly floured work surface, roll each half into a large rectangle. Spread ½ cup grated cheddar cheese and ½ of the diced green onions on dough. Roll jelly-roll fashion (see page 9) and pinch tightly to seal closed. Place seam side down on a greased baking sheet, cover and let rise for about 45 minutes. Bake in a preheated 350° oven for 15 to 18 minutes.

per ¹⁄₁₂ recipe 183 calories, 5 g fat (3 g sat fat), 7 g protein, 27 g carbohydrate, 16 mg cholesterol, 161 mg sodium

HERB-FILLED LOAF

Yield: 1 loaf

This recipe uses a very easy, basic dough that has an herb filling rolled into it for flavor. Vary the herb according to the meal with which it is served —perhaps oregano and/or basil with Italian entrées, cilantro with Mexican or Oriental flavors.

DOUGH
1 cup water
1 tsp. sugar
½ tsp. salt
3 cups all-purpose flour
1½ tsp. rapid or quick yeast

FILLING
1 tbs. dried herbs, or 3 tbs. chopped fresh
⅓ cup nonfat *Yogurt Cheese*, follows

Mix herbs into *Yogurt Cheese* and set aside. Remove dough from the bread machine upon completion of the dough cycle. Roll dough into a large rectangle on a lightly floured work surface. Spread filling on top of dough and roll jelly-roll fashion, starting on the wide side (see page 9). Cut into 12 equal pieces and place in greased muffin cups. Cover with a kitchen towel and let rise in a warm, draft-free location for 30 minutes. Bake in a preheated 350° oven for 15 minutes or until golden brown.

per 1/12 **recipe**   *124 calories, 1 g fat (0 g sat fat), 4 g protein, 26 g carbohydrate, 0 mg cholesterol, 100 mg sodium*

YOGURT CHEESE

Coffee filters and a small colander work just as well as the yogurt cheese makers available in some stores. Place two or three layers of coffee filters in a small colander and place the colander on top of a small bowl. Put nonfat yogurt (without gelatin — check the label) into the colander and refrigerate for 2 to 10 hours. The whey will separate from the yogurt and drain into the bowl beneath it. The remaining yogurt will be very thick and may be used as a substitute for cream cheese in many recipes. The whey may be disposed of or may be refrigerated and included in 1 to 2 teaspoon portions with the liquid for bread baking as a dough enhancer. The yield from yogurt is usually about half: 4 cups yogurt yields about 2 cups *Yogurt Cheese*.

POTATO RYE CHEESE ROLLS

Yield: 12 rolls

Because rye grows so well in the northern climes of Europe, it is a staple in their bread making. Many ryes, like Dutch Roggerbrood or some German ryes, use potatoes; this recipe uses potato flakes for ease. Because of the high percentage of rye flour, it is necessary to allow the rolls to rise longer than normal. This dough should be moist and will be slightly sticky. Take care not to add too much flour, which produces a heavier roll. Instead, spray your hands and the work surface with a nonstick vegetable spray. These rolls may be made with or without the cheese filling. The cocoa and coffee are used to give the bread a darker color. Start with 1½ cups flour and add more if necessary to obtain the right consistency.

DOUGH

1 cup water
2 tbs. vegetable oil
3 tbs. molasses or honey
2 tbs. brown sugar
1 tsp. salt
1 tbs. unsweetened cocoa
1 tbs. instant coffee granules

1-2 tbs. caraway or other seeds
½ cup rye flour
½ cup whole wheat flour
½ cup instant potato flakes
1½-1¾ cups bread flour
2 tsp. rapid or quick yeast

FILLING
twelve ½- or 1-inch cubes very sharp cheddar cheese

WASH
cold water

TOPPING
caraway seeds or favorite seeds

Grease hands and work surface (rather than flouring) and remove dough from the machine upon completion of the dough cycle. Divide dough into 12 equal pieces. Form dough into balls and stuff each one with cheese cube (see page 11). Pinch ends together to seal in cheese and place on a greased baking sheet, or perforated pizza pan for a crustier roll. Cover and let rise in a warm, draft-free location for 1 to 1½ hours. Brush or spray rolls with a cold water wash and sprinkle with seeds. Bake in a preheated 350° oven for 15 to 20 minutes. Cool slightly in pans and remove to a rack to finish cooling.

per ¹⁄₁₂ *recipe*   *161 calories, 5 g fat (2 g sat fat), 5 g protein, 24 g carbohydrate, 7 mg cholesterol, 230 mg sodium*

CHEESE-FILLED HERB ROLLS

Yield: 12 rolls

These simple-to-make rolls make a great accompaniment to soup or salad for a light meal. While the recipe calls for basil, use mint, oregano or cilantro (or any favorite herb) as a variation. I particularly like basil with mozzarella and mint with feta. Of course, there is also cheddar with cilantro...

DOUGH
1 cup water
2 tbs. olive oil
1 clove or 1 tsp. minced garlic
1 tbs. sugar
½ tsp. salt
¼ cup chopped fresh basil, or 1 tbs. dried
3 cups bread flour
1½ tsp. rapid or quick yeast

FILLING
2 cups (8 oz.) grated mozzarella or crumbled feta cheese

WASH
cold water or olive oil

Remove dough from the machine upon completion of the dough cycle and divide into 12 equal pieces. On a lightly floured work surface, roll each piece into a 6- or 7-inch round. Place about 2 tbs. cheese in the center of each round. Fold sides over to center, encasing cheese, and press firmly to seal closed (see page 11). Place seam side down on a greased baking sheet, cover and let rise for about 1 hour. Just before baking, pierce top of dough with the tines of a fork and brush with water for a crusty exterior, or olive oil for a softer crust. Bake in a preheated 350° oven for about 15 minutes.

per ¹⁄₁₂ recipe   *174 calories, 6 g fat (2 g sat fat), 8 g protein, 22 g carbohydrate, 11 mg cholesterol, 178 mg sodium*

HERB ROLLS

Yield: 12-15 rolls

These herb rolls make great sandwich or dinner rolls. Experiment with some of the flavored olive oils (garlic, jalapeño, etc.), found in grocery stores, for added flavor. Use any shape described on pages 5-12.

1⅓ cups water
2 tbs. olive oil
1 tbs. sugar
1 tsp. salt
1 clove or 1 tsp. minced garlic

1 tsp. black pepper
1 tbs. dried basil, or ¼ cup chopped
 fresh
4 cups bread flour
2 tsp. rapid or quick yeast

Remove dough from the machine upon completion of the dough cycle and place on a lightly floured work surface. Divide dough into 12 to 15 equal pieces, shape into small balls and place on a lightly greased baking sheet. Cover with a kitchen towel and let rise for about 1 hour in a warm, draft-free location. Bake in a preheated 350° oven for 15 to 20 minutes.

per ¹⁄₁₂ recipe   160 calories, 3 g fat (0 g sat fat), 5 g protein, 29 g carbohydrate, 0 mg cholesterol, 179 mg sodium

OLIVE WALNUT BREAD

Yield: 1 loaf

Carol Neel serves this festive bread at holiday meals. If you have whole olives, slice them to fill ½ to ¾ cup. Begin with 1¼ cups water and add more as needed.

DOUGH

1¼-1⅓ cups water
3 tbs. olive oil
1 tsp. sugar
1 tsp. salt

½ tsp. black pepper
4 cups all-purpose flour
2 tsp. rapid or quick yeast

FILLING

1 can (3.8 oz.) sliced black olives

½ cup chopped walnuts

Remove dough from the machine upon completion of the dough cycle. On a lightly floured work surface, roll dough into a large rectangle. Sprinkle dough with olives and walnuts. Roll jelly-roll fashion, beginning on the short side (see page 9). Pinch seams to seal and place seam side down on a greased baking sheet, tucking ends under. With a sharp knife or razor, cut several ⅛-inch-deep slashes in top of loaf. Cover with a kitchen towel and let rise in a warm, draft-free location for about 20 minutes. Bake in a preheated 400° oven for 20 to 25 minutes or until bread sounds hollow when tapped. Cool on a wire rack and cut into thin slices to serve.

per ¹⁄₁₂ recipe   227 calories, 8 g fat (1 g sat fat), 5 g protein, 34 g carbohydrate, 0 mg cholesterol, 258 mg sodium

HERBED MONKEY BREAD

Turn a simple spaghetti meal into a special feast with the addition of this bread. Serve it whole and allow guests to help themselves by pulling off a portion.

DOUGH

1⅛ cups water
2 tbs. olive oil
1 tsp. sugar
½ tsp. salt

1 tbs. dried oregano, or 3 tbs. fresh
3 cups bread flour
2 tsp. rapid or quick yeast

ADDITIONAL INGREDIENTS

⅓ cup olive oil
1 cup freshly grated Parmesan cheese

Remove dough from the machine upon completion of the dough cycle. Break off pieces of dough to form as many 1-inch balls as possible. Roll balls in olive oil and then in cheese. Place balls in a greased Bundt baking pan. If there is any remaining oil, pour it on top of balls and sprinkle with remaining cheese. Cover and let rise for about 1 hour. Bake in a preheated 350° oven for 30 to 35 minutes.

per ¹⁄₁₂ *recipe with additional ingredients* 214 calories, 11 g fat (3 g sat fat), 7 g protein, 21 g carbohydrate, 7 mg cholesterol, 245 mg sodium

SIMPLE BAGUETTES

Yield: 2 large or 3 medium baguettes

Whether from Italy, France or Cuba, baguettes share two things: their long, slender shape and the fact that they contain no oil. Because there is no oil, they are best eaten when very fresh. Generate steam for a crisp crust (see pages 14 and 15).

DOUGH
1½ cups water
1 tbs. sugar
1 tsp. salt
4 cups bread flour
2 tsp. rapid or quick yeast

WASH
cold water

TOPPING
sesame seeds, poppy seeds or other
   favorite seeds, optional

Remove dough from the machine upon completion of the dough cycle and divide in half. On a cornmeal-covered work surface (to prevent sticking), roll each portion of dough into a large rectangle. Roll dough jelly-roll fashion, beginning on the wide side (see page 9). Place on a greased, cornmeal-covered baguette pan or baking sheet to rise for 1 to 1½ hours. Just before baking, slash top of bread with a razor blade or very sharp knife. Wash with cold water and top with seeds if desired. Bake in a preheated 400° oven for about 15 minutes until bread is brown and sounds hollow when tapped.

per 1/12 *recipe*   *139 calories, 0 g fat (0 g sat fat), 5 g protein, 28 g carbohydrate, 0 mg cholesterol, 179 mg sodium*

SPONGE BAGUETTES

Yield: 2 medium baguettes

The flavor of bread is developed as the dough rises and rests. The sponge allows the bread to develop a more distinct flavor as it rests for several hours or, better still, overnight. Use any of the techniques for developing a crisp crust found on pages 14 and 15.

SPONGE*
1 cup water
2 cups bread flour
1 tsp. rapid or quick yeast

DOUGH
*sponge
1 tbs. sugar
1 tsp. salt
1 cup bread flour
1 tsp. rapid or quick yeast
1-2 tbs. water if necessary

WASH
cold water

TOPPING
poppy seeds, sesame seeds or other
  favorite seeds, optional

Add sponge ingredients to the machine pan, start machine and allow it to knead for 5 to 10 minutes. Turn off machine and allow sponge to sit undisturbed in pan for 6 to 10 hours. If you have a Welbilt, DAK or Citizen machine or if your machine is otherwise occupied, mix sponge in a large bowl, cover with plastic wrap and allow to sit undisturbed in a warm, draft-free location for 6 to 10 hours.

After 6 to 10 hours, add remaining ingredients, except water, to sponge and start the dough cycle. Allow dough to knead for a few minutes and then add 1 to 2 tbs. water to soften dough if necessary. Remove dough from machine upon completion of the dough cycle. Divide dough in half and roll each half into a large rectangle. Beginning on the wide side, roll jelly-roll fashion (see page 9) into baguette shapes. Place on a greased, cornmeal-covered baguette pan or baking sheet to rise for 1 to 1½ hours. Just before baking, wash or spray bread with cold water, slash top with a razor blade or very sharp knife and sprinkle with seeds if desired. Bake in a preheated 400° oven for 20 to 25 minutes until bread is brown and sounds hollow when tapped.

per ¹⁄₁₂ *recipe*   *105 calories, 1 g fat (0 g sat fat), 4 g protein, 21 g carbohydrate, 0 mg cholesterol, 178 mg sodium*

MEXICAN-FLAVORED BAGUETTES OR BREADSTICKS

Yield: 2 baguettes
or 24 breadsticks

Use these delightful breads to scoop up your favorite salsa. Masa harina may be found in Mexican groceries, through mail order companies or in some large grocery stores. It may be found under the name "maseca." Generate steam for a crisp crust with techniques from pages 14 and 15.

DOUGH
1⅓ cups water
2 tbs. olive oil
1-2 tsp. diced jalapeños, or to taste
2-4 tbs. chopped fresh cilantro
1 tbs. sugar

1 tsp. salt
½ cup masa harina
3 cups bread flour
1½ tsp. rapid or quick yeast

WASH
cold water

TOPPING
coarse salt, optional

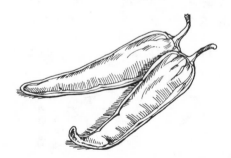

For baguettes: Remove dough from the machine upon completion of the dough cycle and divide in half. Roll dough into 2 large rectangles on a cornmeal-covered work surface to prevent sticking. Roll dough jelly-roll fashion, beginning on the wide side (see page 9). Place on a greased, cornmeal-covered baguette pan or baking sheet to rise for 45 to 60 minutes. Just before baking, slash top of bread with a razor blade or very sharp knife. Wash or spray with cold water and bake in a preheated 400° oven for about 15 minutes until bread is brown and sounds hollow when tapped.

For breadsticks: Remove dough from the machine upon completion of the dough cycle. Divide into 24 equal pieces. Roll each piece into a thin rope about 6 to 8 inches long. Place on a lightly greased baking sheet (or perforated pizza pan for a crisper stick), cover and let rise in a warm, draft-free location for about 15 minutes. Brush or spray with cold water and sprinkle with coarse salt if desired. Bake in a preheated 400° oven for 10 to 15 minutes. The longer they bake, the crisper they will be. Do not store in plastic wrap, as they will soften.

per 1/24 *recipe*   71 calories, 2 g fat (0 g sat fat), 2 g protein, 12 g carbohydrate, 0 mg cholesterol, 91 mg sodium

JALAPEÑO CHEESE CORNMEAL BAGUETTES OR BREADSTICKS

Yield: 2 baguettes
or 24 breadsticks

Dip these breadsticks into salsa instead of using tortilla chips. These are similar to Mexican-flavored baguettes or breadsticks, but use easy-to-find cornmeal instead of the masa harina. Generate steam for a crisp crust (see pages 14 and 15).

DOUGH

1¼ cups water
2 tbs. olive oil
½ cup shredded cheddar cheese
1-2 jalapeños, diced, or to taste
1 tsp. sugar
½ tsp. salt

¼ tsp. cayenne pepper
½ cup cornmeal
3 cups bread flour
1½ tsp. rapid or quick yeast

WASH
cold water

TOPPING
coarse salt, optional

For baguettes: Remove dough from the machine upon completion of the dough cycle and divide in half. Roll dough into 2 large rectangles on a cornmeal-covered work surface to prevent sticking. Roll dough jelly-roll fashion, beginning on the wide side (see page 9). Place on a greased, cornmeal-covered baguette pan or baking sheet to rise for 45 to 60 minutes. Just before baking, slash top of bread with a razor blade or very sharp knife. Wash or spray with cold water and bake in a preheated 400° oven for about 15 minutes until bread is brown and sounds hollow when tapped.

For breadsticks: Remove dough from the machine upon completion of the dough cycle. Divide into 24 equal pieces. Roll each piece into a thin rope about 6 to 8 inches long. Place on a lightly greased baking sheet (or perforated pizza pan for a crisper stick), cover and let rise in a warm, draft-free location for about 15 minutes. Brush or spray with cold water and sprinkle with coarse salt if desired. Bake in a preheated 400° oven for 10 to 15 minutes. The longer they bake, the crisper they will be. Do not store in plastic wrap, as they will soften.

per 1/24 *recipe*   *252 calories, 2 g fat (1 g sat fat), 3 g protein, 12 g carbohydrate, 2 mg cholesterol, 65 mg sodium*

ORANGE GINGER BAGUETTES OR BREADSTICKS

Yield: 2 baguettes
or 24 breadsticks

Serve these Oriental-flavored breadsticks with soups or salads. Fresh, finely chopped ginger root is best, but ginger packed in jars, sold in the produce section of large grocery stores, is an acceptable substitute. See pages 14 and 15 for methods of steaming to form a crisp crust.

DOUGH
1⅛ cups orange juice
2 tbs. olive oil
1 clove or 1 tsp. minced garlic
1 tsp. grated ginger root, or to taste
1 tbs. sugar

1 tsp. salt
1 tsp. coarsely ground black pepper
3 cups bread flour
1½ tsp. rapid or quick yeast

WASH
cold water

TOPPING
coarse salt, optional

For baguettes: Remove dough from the machine upon completion of the dough cycle and divide in half. Roll dough into 2 large rectangles on a cornmeal-covered work surface to prevent sticking. Roll dough jelly-roll fashion, beginning on the wide side (see page 9). Place on a greased, cornmeal-covered baguette pan or baking sheet to rise for 45 to 60 minutes. Just before baking, slash top of bread with a razor blade or very sharp knife. Wash or spray with cold water and bake in a preheated 400° oven for about 15 minutes until bread is brown and sounds hollow when tapped.

For breadsticks: Remove dough from the machine upon completion of the dough cycle. Divide into 24 equal pieces. Roll each piece into a thin rope about 6 to 8 inches long. Place on a lightly greased baking sheet (or perforated pizza pan for a crisper stick), cover and let rise in a warm, draft-free location for about 15 minutes. Brush or spray with cold water and sprinkle with coarse salt if desired. Bake in a preheated 400° oven for 10 to 15 minutes. The longer they bake, the crisper they will be. Do not store in plastic wrap, as they will soften.

per 1/24 *recipe*   68 calories, 1 g fat (0 g sat fat), 2 g protein, 12 g carbohydrate, 0 mg cholesterol, 89 mg sodium

TOMATO HERB BAGUETTES OR BREADSTICKS

Yield: 2 baguettes
or 24 breadsticks

Dried tomatoes should be cut into tiny pieces for this, or use tomato sprinkles if your grocery store carries them. The basil may be increased to taste if desired. Generate steam (pages 14 and 15) for a crisp crust.

DOUGH

1⅛ cups water
2 tbs. olive oil
1 clove or 1 tsp. minced garlic
1 tbs. sugar
1 tsp. salt

¼ cup coarsely chopped dried tomatoes
1-2 tbs. chopped fresh basil, or 1-2 tsp. dried
3 cups bread flour
1½ tsp. rapid or quick yeast

WASH

cold water

TOPPING

coarse salt, optional

For baguettes: Remove dough from the machine upon completion of the dough cycle and divide in half. Roll dough into 2 large rectangles on a cornmeal-covered work surface to prevent sticking. Roll dough jelly-roll fashion, beginning on the wide side (see page 9). Place on a greased, cornmeal-covered baguette pan or baking sheet to rise for 45 to 60 minutes. Just before baking, slash top of bread with a razor blade or very sharp knife. Wash or spray with cold water and bake in a preheated 400° oven for about 15 minutes until bread is brown and sounds hollow when tapped.

For breadsticks: Remove dough from the machine upon completion of the dough cycle. Divide into 24 equal pieces. Roll each piece into a thin rope about 6 to 8 inches long. Place on a lightly greased baking sheet (or perforated pizza pan for a crisper stick), cover and let rise in a warm, draft-free location for about 15 minutes. Brush or spray with cold water and sprinkle with coarse salt if desired. Bake in a preheated 400° oven for 10 to 15 minutes. The longer they bake, the crisper they will be. Do not store in plastic wrap, as they will soften.

per 1/24 *recipe*   64 calories, 1 g fat (0 g sat fat), 2 g protein, 11 g carbohydrate, 0 mg cholesterol, 90 mg sodium

PARMESAN PEPPER BAGUETTES OR BREADSTICKS

Yield: 2 baguettes
or 24 breadsticks

A twist on an Italian herb bread, this bread uses freshly grated Parmesan cheese. In a pinch, the grated Parmesan cheese found in the refrigerated cheese section may be used, but do not use the "green can" cheese. Use either freshly ground pepper or the coarse grind as found in the grocery store. Generate steam (see pages 14 and 15) for a crisp crust.

DOUGH
1⅛ cups water
1 tbs. olive oil
½ cup grated Parmesan cheese
1 tbs. sugar

1 tsp. salt
1 tsp. coarsely ground black pepper
3 cups bread flour
2 tsp. rapid or quick yeast

WASH
cold water

TOPPING
coarse salt, optional

For baguettes: Remove dough from the machine upon completion of the dough cycle and divide in half. Roll dough into 2 large rectangles on a cornmeal-covered work surface to prevent sticking. Roll dough jelly-roll fashion, beginning on the wide side (see page 9). Place on a greased, cornmeal-covered baguette pan or baking sheet to rise for 45 to 60 minutes. Just before baking, slash top of bread with a razor blade or very sharp knife. Wash or spray with cold water and bake in a preheated 400° oven for about 15 minutes until bread is brown and sounds hollow when tapped.

For breadsticks: Remove dough from the machine upon completion of the dough cycle. Divide into 24 equal pieces. Roll each piece into a thin rope about 6 to 8 inches long. Place on a lightly greased baking sheet (or perforated pizza pan for a crisper stick), cover and let rise in a warm, draft-free location for about 15 minutes. Brush or spray with cold water and sprinkle with coarse salt if desired. Bake in a preheated 400° oven for 10 to 15 minutes. The longer they bake, the crisper they will be. Do not store in plastic wrap, as they will soften.

per 1/24 *recipe*   *67 calories, 1 g fat (1 g sat fat), 3 g protein, 11 g carbohydrate, 2 mg cholesterol, 128 mg sodium*

ITALIAN BREADSTICKS (GRISSINI)

Enjoy these rustic variations of plain breadsticks with a hearty bottle of wine and chunks of cheese.

DOUGH
1 cup milk
2 tbs. butter or margarine
1 tsp. sugar
½ tsp. salt
3 cups all-purpose flour
1½ tsp. rapid or quick yeast

ADDITIONAL INGREDIENTS
about ½ cup milk
about ¼ cup sesame seeds

Remove dough from the machine upon completion of the dough cycle. Divide dough into about 24 pieces. Roll each piece into a thin rope 6 to 8 inches long. Dip each one into milk (in a bowl) and then roll in seeds on a plate or piece of waxed paper. Place about 1 inch apart on a greased baking sheet and immediately bake in a preheated 450° oven for 10 to 12 minutes or until golden brown. Do not store in plastic wrap, as they will soften.

per 1/24 ***recipe with added ingredients*** *80 calories, 2 g fat (0 g sat fat), 2 g protein, 13 g carbohydrate, 3 mg cholesterol, 53 mg sodium*

PRETZELS

Yield: 10 pretzels

These soft pretzels are best eaten warm or reheated. As a variation, sprinkle the pretzels with any favorite seed instead of the salt.

DOUGH
1⅛ cups water
2 tsp. sugar
½ tsp. salt
3 cups all-purpose flour
1½ tsp. rapid or quick yeast

ADDITIONAL INGREDIENTS
2 qt. water, plus 2 tbs. baking soda

WASH
1 egg beaten with 1 tbs. water

TOPPING
coarse salt or seeds

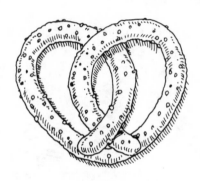

Remove dough from the machine upon completion of the dough cycle. Divide it into 10 equal pieces and roll each one into a long rope, 15 to 20 inches. If you have trouble rolling ropes that long, let them rest for about 5 or 10 minutes and then roll out again. After ropes are formed, shape them into pretzels (see page 11), place on a lightly greased baking sheet, cover and let rise for 20 to 30 minutes. Meanwhile, bring 2 quarts water to a boil in a large, nonaluminum pan and stir in baking soda. Reduce heat slightly so that water is just below a boil. With a large slotted spoon, gently place 2 or 3 pretzels at a time into water and cook for about 30 seconds on each side. Remove from water and return to greased baking sheet. Brush with egg wash, sprinkle with salt or seeds and bake in a preheated 450° oven for 10 to 12 minutes or until golden and crusty.

per 1/10 *recipe*   *141 calories, 0 g fat (0 g sat fat), 4 g protein, 30 g carbohydrate, 0 mg cholesterol, 108 mg sodium*

BEER BREADSTICKS

The beer does not have to be flat, but it should be warmed in the microwave for 30 to 60 seconds. Add water if you don't have quite enough beer.

DOUGH
1⅛ cups beer
1 tbs. vegetable oil
1 tsp. sugar

½ tsp. salt
3 cups all-purpose flour
1½ tsp. rapid or quick yeast

WASH
cold water

TOPPING
coarse salt or seeds of choice

Remove dough from the machine upon completion of the dough cycle. Divide dough into 20 to 24 pieces. Roll each piece into a rope about 6 to 8 inches long. Place about 1 inch apart on a greased baking sheet, brush or spray with cold water, sprinkle with coarse salt or seeds, and immediately bake in a preheated 450° oven for 10 to 12 minutes or until golden brown. Do not store in plastic wrap, as they will soften.

per 1/24 recipe   68 calories, 1 g fat (0 g sat fat), 2 g protein, 13 g carbohydrate, 0 mg cholesterol, 45 mg sodium

SWEET ROLLS AND COFFEE CAKES

SWEET ROLLS 52
SWEET MONKEY BREAD . . 53
CINNAMON BUNS 54
ORANGE CRAISIN BUNS . . 56
CARAMEL ALMOND BUNS . . 58
POTATO CINNAMON ROLLS . 60
WALNUT RAISIN CINNAMON
      ROLLS 61
STICKY BUNS 62
HONEY BUNS 64
DOUBLE CHOCOLATE ROLLS . 65
COCONUT CHOCOLATE ROLLS 66
SWEDISH CHOCOLATE BREAD 67

MEXICAN CHOCOLATE ROLLS 68
PUMPKIN ROLLS 69
HAWAIIAN NUT CRESCENTS . 70
LEMON CRESCENTS 72
POPPY SEED-FILLED ROLLS . 74
GERMAN COFFEE CRESCENTS 76
GERMAN SOUR CREAM SWEET
      ROLLS 78
MORAVIAN COFFEE CAKE . . 80
GERMAN COFFEE CAKE . . . 81
STREUSEL-TOPPED COFFEE
      CAKE 82
SOUR CREAM COFFEE CAKE . 84

SWEET ROLLS

These sweet rolls are a delightful treat for breakfast, sandwiches or dinner. Make ordinary shapes (below) or use any of the fancy variations on pages 5-12. Add food coloring to the liquids for a decorative touch. For a sweeter treat, glaze rolls (see **Finishing Touches**, *page 156) while still warm instead of washing with the egg.*

DOUGH
1⅛ cups milk
2 tbs. butter or margarine
1 egg, large
¼ cup sugar

1 tsp. salt
4 cups all-purpose flour
2 tsp. rapid or quick yeast

WASH
1 egg beaten with 1-2 tbs. milk or cream

Remove dough from the machine upon completion of the dough cycle and place on a lightly floured work surface. Divide dough into 12 equal pieces, shape into desired roll shape or small balls, and place on a lightly greased baking sheet. Cover with a kitchen towel and let rise for about 1 hour in a warm, draft-free location. Brush with egg-milk wash. Bake in a preheated 350° oven for 15 to 20 minutes.

per roll, ¹⁄₁₂ *recipe* 201 calories, 3 g fat (1 g sat fat), 5 g protein, 37 g carbohydrate, 23 mg cholesterol, 196 mg sodium

52   SWEET ROLLS AND COFFEE CAKES

SWEET MONKEY BREAD

Yield: 1 loaf

There are hundreds of variations on monkey breads, or "pull-aparts," but this is one of my favorites. Serve whole and pull off a portion to eat. Great fun!

DOUGH

1⅛ cups milk
2 tbs. butter or margarine
1 egg, large
1 tsp. vanilla extract

¼ cup sugar
1 tsp. salt
4 cups all-purpose flour
2 tsp. rapid or quick yeast

ADDITIONAL INGREDIENTS

6 tbs. butter, melted
1 cup very finely chopped nuts

Remove dough from the machine upon completion of the dough cycle. Form as many 1-inch balls as possible. Roll balls in melted butter and then in chopped nuts. Place balls in a greased tube pan or Bundt pan. If there is any remaining melted butter, pour it on top of balls and sprinkle with any remaining nuts. Cover and let rise for about 1 hour. Bake in a preheated 350° oven for 30 to 35 minutes.

per 1/12 *recipe with additional ingredients* *316 calories, 15 g fat (6 g sat fat), 7 g protein, 39g carbohydrate, 38 mg cholesterol, 198 mg sodium*

CINNAMON BUNS

This traditional recipe for a simple cinnamon bun is always a winner.

DOUGH
¾ cup milk
2 tbs. butter or margarine
1 egg, large
2 tbs. sugar
1 tsp. salt
3 cups all-purpose flour
2 tsp. rapid or quick yeast

FILLING
1 tbs. butter, melted
¼ cup sugar
1 tbs. cinnamon
½ cup raisins
¼ cup chopped walnuts

GLAZE
Powdered Sugar Glaze, page 158, optional

Remove dough from the machine upon completion of the dough cycle and roll into a rectangle on a floured work surface. Add only enough flour to prevent sticking. Brush dough with melted butter. Mix sugar and cinnamon together and spread evenly over dough. Sprinkle with raisins and nuts. Roll dough jelly-roll fashion (see page 9), beginning on the wide side. Cut into 12 equal slices and place in greased muffin cups. Cover and let rise in a warm, draft-free location for 30 to 45 minutes. Bake in a preheated 350° oven for 20 to 30 minutes or until golden brown. Glaze while warm if desired.

per 1/12 *recipe*   *214 calories, 5 g fat (2 g sat fat), 5 g protein, 37 g carbohydrate, 26 mg cholesterol, 193 mg sodium*

ORANGE CRAISIN BUNS

Yield: 12 buns

Craisins are dried, sweetened cranberries available from large grocery stores, gourmet shops or mail order catalogs. Sometimes they are called "crannies." For variety, use any favorite dried fruit (apricots, cherries, etc.).

DOUGH
1⅛ cups orange juice
2 tbs. butter or margarine
1 egg, large
1 tbs. sugar
1 tsp. salt
1 tsp. dried orange peel, or freshly grated to taste
3 cups all-purpose flour
2 tsp. rapid or quick yeast

FILLING
1 tbs. butter, melted
¼ cup sugar
1-2 tsp. dried orange peel, or freshly grated to taste
½ cup dried cranberries
¼ cup finely chopped almonds

GLAZE
Orange Glaze, page 158, optional

Remove dough from the machine upon completion of the dough cycle and roll into a rectangle on a floured work surface. Add only enough flour to prevent sticking. Brush dough with melted butter. Mix sugar and orange peel together and spread evenly over dough. Sprinkle with dried cranberries (or other dried fruit) and nuts. Roll dough jelly-roll fashion, beginning on the wide side (see page 9). Cut into 12 equal slices and place in greased muffin cups. Cover and let rise in a warm, draft-free location for 30 to 45 minutes. Bake in a preheated 350° oven for 20 to 30 minutes or until golden brown. Glaze while warm if desired.

per 1/12 *recipe*   *215 calories, 5 g fat (2 g sat fat), 5 g protein, 38 g carbohydrate, 25 mg cholesterol, 186 mg sodium*

CARAMEL ALMOND BUNS

These are sinfully rich and are a definite "must try."

DOUGH
¾ cup milk
2 tbs. butter or margarine
1 egg, large
1 tsp. almond extract
2 tbs. sugar
1 tsp. salt
3 cups all-purpose flour
2 tsp. rapid or quick yeast

FILLING
2 tbs. butter, melted
¼ cup brown sugar, firmly packed
1 tsp. almond extract
½ cup finely chopped almonds

GLAZE
Powdered Sugar Glaze with almond extract, page 158, optional

Remove dough from the machine upon completion of the dough cycle and roll into a rectangle on a floured work surface. Add only enough flour to prevent sticking. Mix together melted butter, brown sugar and almond extract and spread evenly over dough. Sprinkle with almonds. Roll dough jelly-roll fashion, beginning on the wide side (see page 9). Cut into 12 equal slices and place in greased muffin cups. Cover and let rise in a warm, draft-free location for 30 to 45 minutes. Bake in a preheated 350° oven for 20 to 30 minutes or until golden brown. Glaze while warm if desired.

per 1/12 **recipe**   *218 calories, 7 g fat (3 g sat fat), 6 g protein, 32 g carbohydrate, 28 mg cholesterol, 195 mg sodium*

POTATO CINNAMON ROLLS

Yield: 12 rolls

Use regular baking or sweet potatoes for this delightful cinnamon roll variation.

DOUGH
1/2 cup mashed potatoes
1/2 cup milk
1 egg
2 tbs. butter or margarine
1 tsp. vanilla extract
1/4 cup sugar
1/2 tsp. salt
3-3 1/2 cups all-purpose flour
1 1/2 tsp. rapid or quick yeast

FILLING
2 tbs. butter, melted
1 tbs. cinnamon
1/2 cup raisins, or dried fruit of choice
1/3 cup chopped walnuts or pecans

GLAZE
Powdered Sugar Glaze, page 158, optional

Remove dough from the machine upon completion of the dough cycle. On a lightly floured work surface, roll dough into a large rectangle. Brush with melted butter and sprinkle with cinnamon. Spread raisins and nuts on top and roll tightly, jelly-roll fashion, beginning on the wide side (see page 9). Cut into 12 equal slices and place in lightly greased muffin cups. Cover and let rise for about 1 hour in a warm, draft-free location. Bake in a preheated 350° oven for 15 to 20 minutes. Glaze while warm if desired.

per 1/12 recipe   267 calories, 7 g fat (3 g sat fat), 11g protein, 42 g carbohydrate, 28 mg cholesterol, 137 mg sodium

WALNUT RAISIN CINNAMON ROLLS

Enjoy these for breakfast or a mid-afternoon snack. Walnut oil adds flavor, but any vegetable oil may be used. Vary shaping with ideas on pages 5-12.

DOUGH

1⅓ cups milk
¼ cup sugar
2 tbs. walnut or vegetable oil
1 tsp. vanilla extract
1 tsp. salt

1 tsp. cinnamon
4 cups all-purpose flour
2 tsp. rapid or quick yeast
ADD: ½ cup raisins
ADD: ¼ cup chopped walnuts

WASH

1 egg beaten with 1-2 tbs. milk or cream

Add raisins and nuts after the machine kneads for about 5 minutes regardless of what machine you have. Remove dough from machine upon completion of the dough cycle and place on a lightly floured work surface. Form dough into 12 small balls and place in lightly greased muffin cups. Cover and let rise for about 1 hour in a warm, draft-free location. Brush with wash. Bake in a preheated 350° oven for 15 to 20 minutes.

per ¹⁄₁₂ *recipe* *253 calories, 6 g fat (1 g sat fat), 6 g protein, 44 g carbohydrate, 1 mg cholesterol, 195 mg sodium*

STICKY BUNS

These traditional American sticky buns are not just for holiday breakfasts! You can also make this recipe in greased muffin cups — just divide topping evenly into 12 cups and place rolls on top.

DOUGH
1 cup milk
1 egg
¼ cup brown sugar, firmly packed
½ tsp. salt
1 tsp. cinnamon
3 cups all-purpose flour
1½ tsp. rapid or quick yeast

FILLING AND TOPPING
6 tbs. butter or margarine, melted
¾ cup brown sugar, firmly packed
½-1 tsp. cinnamon
¼ cup raisins, dried cranberries or other favorite dried fruit
½ cup chopped pecans

Make filling while dough is rising in the machine. Mix together butter, brown sugar and cinnamon; divide in half and set aside.

Remove dough from machine upon completion of the dough cycle. Roll dough into a large rectangle. Spread half of the filling on top of dough, sprinkle evenly with raisins and nuts and roll tightly, jelly-roll fashion, beginning on the wide side (see page 9). Spread remaining filling on the bottom of an 8- or 9-inch round cake pan. Cut dough into 12 equal slices and place on top of mixture. Cover with a kitchen towel and let rise for about 1 hour in a warm, draft-free location. Bake in a preheated 350° oven for 15 to 20 minutes. Cool for about 5 minutes in pan and then turn pan upside down on a large plate or platter. Serve sticky side up.

per 1/12 **recipe**   *306 calories, 10 g fat (4 g sat fat), 5 g protein, 51 g carbohydrate, 34 mg cholesterol, 114 mg sodium*

HONEY BUNS

This is a combination of a sticky bun and a cinnamon bun.

DOUGH
1 cup milk
1 egg, large
2 tbs. vegetable oil
2 tbs. honey
1 tsp. salt
4 cups all-purpose flour
2 tsp. rapid or quick yeast

FILLING
2 tbs. butter, melted
$1/2$ cup finely chopped nuts

TOPPING
$1/4$ cup honey mixed with $1/4$ cup soft
   butter

Remove dough from the machine upon completion of the dough cycle and roll into a rectangle on a floured work surface. Add only enough flour to prevent sticking. Brush dough with melted butter and sprinkle nuts evenly over dough. Roll dough jelly-roll fashion, beginning on the wide side (see page 9). Cut into 12 equal slices and place on a lightly greased baking sheet. Cover and let rise in a warm, draft-free location for 30 to 45 minutes. Bake in a preheated 350° oven for 20 to 30 minutes or until golden brown. Immediately spread rolls with honey butter mixture.

***per** $1/12$ **recipe**   302 calories, 12 g fat (4 g sat fat), 7 g protein, 43 g carbohydrate, 34 mg cholesterol, 197 mg sodium*

DOUBLE CHOCOLATE ROLLS

Yield: 12 rolls

Karen Hubachek says that this recipe was inspired by the pain au chocolat eaten after school by children in France. These will disappear quickly.

DOUGH
¾ cup warm milk
1 egg
¼ cup butter or margarine
¼ cup sugar
¾ tsp. salt
½ tsp. cinnamon, or to taste, optional
2 tbs. Dutch-process cocoa
2½ cups bread flour
1 heaping tsp. rapid or quick yeast

FILLING
Hershey Kisses, chocolate chips or any favorite chocolate candy bar

GLAZE
Powdered Sugar Glaze, page 158, optional

Remove dough from the machine upon completion of the dough cycle. If dough is sticky, knead in only enough flour so that it is easily handled. Form dough into 12 equal balls and stuff each one with a piece of chocolate (see page 11). Pinch ends together to seal in chocolate and place in greased muffin cups. Cover and let rise in a warm, draft-free location for 45 to 60 minutes. Bake in a preheated 350° oven for about 15 minutes. Glaze while warm.

per ¹⁄₁₂ *recipe* 295 calories, 14g fat (8 g sat fat), 6 g protein, 38 g carbohydrate, 34 mg cholesterol, 180 mg sodium

COCONUT CHOCOLATE ROLLS

Yield: 12 rolls

*The combination of coconut and chocolate is delicious. Top with **Coconut Glaze**, page 159, for an even richer roll.*

DOUGH

⅞ cup (7 oz.) milk
2 tbs. butter or margarine
1 egg, large
1 tsp. coconut extract
2 tbs. sugar

1 tsp. salt
¾ cup coconut flakes
3 cups all-purpose or bread flour
2 tsp. rapid or quick yeast

FILLING

12 Hershey Kisses or 1 oz. pieces chocolate

Remove dough from the machine upon completion of the dough cycle. If the dough is sticky, knead in only enough flour so that it is easily handled and divide into 12 equal pieces. Form into 12 balls and stuff each one with a Hershey Kiss or similar size piece of chocolate. Pinch ends together to seal in chocolate (see page 11) and place on a greased baking sheet or in greased muffin cups. Cover and let rise in a warm, draft-free location for 45 to 60 minutes. Bake in a preheated 350° oven for about 15 minutes. Cool slightly in pans and then remove to cool on a rack.

per** 1/12 **recipe *201 calories, 6 g fat (4 g sat fat), 5 g protein, 32 g carbohydrate, 24 mg cholesterol, 210 mg sodium*

SWEDISH CHOCOLATE BREAD

This is traditionally filled with a chocolate filling and chopped hazelnuts. For ease and simplicity, I use Nutella chocolate hazelnut filling found in large grocery stores or kitchen specialty shops. This bread is also often shaped into a large crescent.

DOUGH
1 cup warm milk
1/2 cup butter or margarine
1/4 cup sugar
1/2 tsp. salt
3 cups bread flour
1 1/2 tsp. rapid or quick yeast

FILLING
1/3-1/2 cup Nutella or similar chocolate
  spread

WASH
1 egg beaten with 1-2 tbs. milk or cream

Remove dough from the machine upon completion of the dough cycle. Roll on a lightly floured work surface into a large rectangle. Spread Nutella filling on middle third of dough. With scissors, a sharp knife, pastry or pizza wheel, cut 1-inch strips down both sides of dough from filling to edge. Fold the top of filled center over dough and then alternate fold side strips over filling, angling each folded strip down (see Mock braid, page 10). Place on a greased baking sheet, cover and let rise for about 1 hour. Brush with egg wash and bake in a preheated 350° oven for 20 to 25 minutes.

*per 1/12 **recipe** 221 calories, 9 g fat (6 g sat fat), 5 g protein, 30 g carbohydrate, 21 mg cholesterol, 110 mg sodium*

MEXICAN CHOCOLATE ROLLS

Yield: 12 rolls

This roll boasts the traditional Mexican combination of chocolate and cinnamon.

DOUGH
¾ cup milk
2 tbs. butter or margarine
1 egg, large
2 tbs. sugar
1 tsp. salt
1 tbs. unsweetened cocoa
1 tsp. cinnamon
3 cups all-purpose flour
2 tsp. rapid or quick yeast

FILLING
1 tbs. melted butter
¼ cup sugar
1 tbs. unsweetened cocoa
1 tsp. cinnamon
½ cup chopped toasted hazelnuts or
  walnuts

GLAZE
Powdered Sugar Glaze, page 158,
  optional, or dust with confectioners' sugar

Remove dough from the machine upon completion of the dough cycle and roll into a rectangle on a floured work surface. Add only enough flour to prevent sticking. Brush dough with melted butter. Mix sugar, cocoa and cinnamon together. Sprinkle dough with sugar mixture and nuts. Roll dough jelly-roll fashion, beginning on the wide side (see page 9). Cut into 12 equal slices and place in greased muffin cups. Cover and let rise in a warm, draft-free location for 30 to 45 minutes. Bake in a preheated 350° oven for 15 to 20 minutes.

*per ¹⁄₁₂ **recipe*** *210 calories, 7 g fat (2 g sat fat), 5 g protein, 33 g carbohydrate, 21 mg cholesterol, 199 mg sodium*

PUMPKIN ROLLS

These rolls are a rich autumn treat to enjoy any time of the year.

DOUGH
1 cup milk
1 tbs. butter or margarine
1/4 cup sugar
1/2 tsp. salt
1/2-1 tsp. cinnamon
1/2 cup oats
2 1/2 cups bread flour
1 1/2 tsp. rapid or quick yeast

FILLING
1 cup canned pumpkin
1/2 cup brown sugar, firmly packed
1/2 cup raisins, dried cranberries or cherries
1/2 cup chopped walnuts or pecans

GLAZE
Powdered Sugar Glaze with a pinch of cinnamon, page 158, optional

Remove dough from the machine upon completion of the dough cycle and roll into a rectangle on a lightly floured work surface. Add only enough flour to prevent sticking. Mix all filling ingredients together and spread evenly over dough. Roll dough jelly-roll fashion, beginning on the wide side (see page 9). Cut into 12 equal slices and place in greased muffin cups. Cover and let rise in a warm, draft-free location for 30 to 45 minutes. Bake in a preheated 350° oven for 20 to 30 minutes or until golden brown.

per 1/12 *recipe*   223 calories, 5 g fat (1 g sat fat), 5 g protein, 41 g carbohydrate, 3 mg cholesterol, 105 mg sodium

HAWAIIAN NUT CRESCENTS

These tropical-flavored rolls are delicious served with coffee. Use macadamia nuts for the fullest Hawaiian flavor, but walnuts, pecans or Brazil nuts may be substituted as a less expensive alternative. I have a real sweet tooth and love the optional combination of chocolate and coconut — the only problem is that I can't eat just one (or two)! If you don't want to use a glaze, you can wash with an egg beaten with a little milk just before baking.

DOUGH
¾ cup milk
½ cup butter or margarine
1 egg, large
2 tbs. sugar
1 tsp. salt
½ cup coconut flakes
3 cups all-purpose flour
2 tsp. rapid or quick yeast

FILLING
1 tbs. butter
1 tsp. coconut extract
½ cup coarsely chopped macadamia
  nuts
½ cup chocolate chips, optional

GLAZE
Powdered Sugar Glaze with with
  coconut extract, page 158, or
  Coconut Glaze, page 159

Remove dough from the machine upon completion of the dough cycle and roll into a large round on a floured work surface. Add only enough flour to prevent sticking. Melt butter and allow to cool slightly; mix in coconut extract. Brush dough with butter mixture and sprinkle evenly with nuts. With a knife or a pizza wheel, cut round into 8 pieces as you would a pie. If using chocolate chips, divide them evenly among pieces sprinkled around outside (thicker) edge of triangle; this is so the chocolate is firmly rolled inside each crescent to avoid a chocolate leak. Roll each piece from wide end to point, pressing tightly together as you roll, to form a crescent shape (see page 5). Place rolls on a lightly greased baking sheet. Cover and let rise in a warm, draft-free location for 30 to 45 minutes. Bake in a preheated 350° oven for 15 to 20 minutes or until golden brown.

per 1/8 **recipe**   *265 calories, 15 g fat (7 g sat fat), 5 g protein, 29 g carbohydrate, 41 mg cholesterol, 202 mg sodium*

LEMON CRESCENTS

Fresh lemon juice and peel is preferred for the best flavor, but commercially bottled lemon juice and dried peel may be used. You will release more juice from the lemon if you first roll it on the kitchen counter, pushing down on it with the palm of your hand. You can grate the lemon peel (zest) directly into the bread machine pan to taste. Use the higher amount of sugar in the filling for a sweeter crescent.

DOUGH
1 cup water
2 tbs. lemon juice
2 tbs. butter or margarine
1 egg
1/4 cup sugar
1 tsp. salt
1 tsp. dried lemon peel, or freshly
  grated to taste
4 cups all-purpose flour
2 tsp. rapid or quick yeast

FILLING
4 oz. cream cheese, softened
1/4-1/2 cup confectioners' sugar
1 tsp. dried lemon peel, or freshly
  grated to taste

GLAZE
Lemon Glaze, page 160

Remove dough from the machine upon completion of the dough cycle and roll into a large round on a floured work surface. Add only enough flour to prevent sticking. Mix filling ingredients together and spread evenly over the outside half of the dough. (By spreading it on the outside, the filling is better encased in the dough to prevent leaking during baking.) With a knife or a pizza wheel, cut the round into 8 pieces as you would a pie. Roll each piece from the wide end to the point of the triangle, pressing tightly together as you roll, to form a crescent shape (see page 5). Place rolls on a lightly greased baking pan. Cover and let rise in a warm, draft-free location for 30 to 45 minutes. Bake in a preheated 350° oven for 20 to 25 minutes or until golden brown. Glaze while crescents are still hot.

*per ⅛ **recipe*** *351 calories, 9 g fat (5 g sat fat), 9 g protein, 58 g carbohydrate, 50 mg cholesterol, 320 mg sodium*

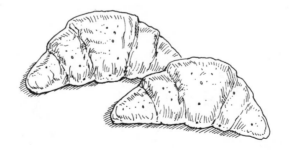

POPPY SEED-FILLED ROLLS

Yield: 12 rolls

Based on a Hungarian stuffed roll, these make great coffee rolls. Begin with 3 cups flour and add more if necessary to form the right consistency.

DOUGH
¾ cup milk
¼ cup butter
2 eggs
2 tbs. sugar
1 tsp. salt
1 tsp. dried lemon peel, or freshly
  grated to taste
3-3¼ cups all-purpose flour
2 tsp. rapid or quick yeast

FILLING
2 tbs. poppy seeds
¼ cup finely ground almonds
1½ tbs. honey

WASH
1 egg beaten with 1 tbs. milk

While dough is rising in the machine, make filling. In a medium bowl, combine poppy seeds and almonds. Add honey; using your hands, mix until all ingredients are moistened and form a doughy consistency; set aside.

Remove dough from machine upon completion of the dough cycle. If dough is sticky, knead in only enough flour so that it is easily handled and divide into 12 equal pieces. Form each piece into a ball and stuff each with a large spoonful of filling (see page 11). Pinch dough together to seal. Place rolls in greased muffin cups or on a baking sheet. Cover and let rise in a warm, draft-free location for about 30 minutes. Brush with egg wash. Bake in a preheated 350° oven for 15 to 20 minutes.

per 1/12 *recipe*   209 calories, 7 g fat (3 g sat fat), 6 g protein, 30 g carbohydrate, 47 mg cholesterol, 198 mg sodium

GERMAN COFFEE CRESCENTS

These coffee crescents are a combination of a filled crescent and a croissant. Bet you can't eat just one! While margarine could be used, butter is preferred.

DOUGH
3/4 cup milk
1 egg
2 tbs. butter
1/4 cup sugar
1 tsp. salt
3 cups all-purpose flour
2 tsp. rapid or quick yeast

ADDITIONAL INGREDIENTS
1/4 cup butter, softened
2 tbs. sugar

FILLING
1/2 cup raisins or chopped dried fruits
  of choice
1/2 cup chopped walnuts
1/4 cup sugar
2 tbs. butter, melted

While dough is rising in the machine, make filling. With a food processor, process dried fruits and nuts until coarsely ground. Add sugar and butter and process until mixture forms a paste. Set aside.

Remove dough from machine upon completion of the dough cycle. Roll dough into a large rectangle on a lightly floured work surface. Spread 2 tbs. of the butter on top of dough and sprinkle with 1 tbs. of the sugar. Fold rectangle into thirds, as you would a letter, and roll into another large rectangle. Spread remaining 2 tbs. butter on top, sprinkle with remaining sugar and fold into thirds again. Fold corners into center to form a ball, turn over and roll dough into a large circle. With a knife, pastry or pizza wheel, cut circle into 8 equal pieces. Place an equal amount of filling mixture on the wide end of each triangle and roll dough from wide end to narrow end to form a crescent (see page 5), tightly pressing and sealing filling inside. Place crescents on a greased baking sheet, cover and let rise for about 30 minutes. Bake in a preheated 350° oven for 20 to 25 minutes or until puffed and golden.

per ⅛ *recipe*   *431 calories, 17 g fat (8 g sat fat), 8 g protein, 62 g carbohydrate, 58 mg cholesterol, 291 mg sodium*

GERMAN SOUR CREAM SWEET ROLLS

Yield: 12-16 rolls

These delightful sweet breads are rolled in sugar and are shaped into small twists or crescents. Keep an eye on the dough and add water if necessary, ½ tbs. at a time, while dough is kneading. Sour cream sometimes makes it necessary to adjust moisture to get the right consistency. This dough should be very soft. Scrape the sides of the pan with a rubber spatula if necessary to help push ingredients towards the kneading paddle.

DOUGH
¾ cup sour cream
2 tbs. butter or margarine
1 egg
1 tsp. vanilla extract
¼ cup sugar
1 tsp. salt
3 cups all-purpose flour
2 tsp. rapid or quick yeast

ADDITIONAL INGREDIENT
½ cup sugar

Warm sour cream in the microwave for 30 to 60 seconds before adding to the machine pan.

Upon completion of the dough cycle, liberally sprinkle sugar on the work surface. Remove dough from machine and press into a large rectangle. Flip dough over several times, coating with sugar to prevent sticking. The dough is so soft that it is easier to press by hand than it is to roll it with a rolling pin. With a knife or a pizza wheel, cut dough into small rectangles as shown. Twist each rectangle into a long spiral and curl into a round, pinching sides closed to seal. Place twisted rounds on a slightly greased baking sheet, cover with a kitchen towel and place in a warm, draft-free location to rise for about 1 hour. Bake in a preheated 350° oven for 20 to 25 minutes or until lightly browned. The twists will be sticky because of the sugar. If they are browning too quickly, cover with a tent made with aluminum foil.

per ¹⁄₁₂ *recipe*   *217 calories, 6 g fat (3 g sat fat), 4 g protein, 37 g carbohydrate, 29 mg cholesterol, 192 mg sodium*

MORAVIAN COFFEE CAKE

Familiar to anyone who has visited the Pennsylvania Dutch area, variations of this popular sweet coffee cake are enjoyed all over the world.

DOUGH
1¼ cups milk
2 tbs. butter or margarine
¼ cup sugar
1 tsp. salt
¼ cup instant potato flakes
3 cups all-purpose flour
1½ tsp. rapid or quick yeast

TOPPING
½ cup firmly packed brown sugar
1 tbs. cinnamon
¼ cup butter, melted

Remove dough from the machine upon completion of the dough cycle and press into a lightly greased 9-x-13-inch baking pan. Make small indentations in dough with your finger, randomly or in a pattern. Mix sugar and cinnamon together and press sugar mixture into indentations. Sprinkle any remaining sugar over the top. Drizzle with melted butter. Cover and let rise in a warm, draft-free location for 45 to 60 minutes, or until almost to top of pan. Bake in a preheated 350° oven until bread is brown and crust is hard, about 25 to 30 minutes. Cool on a wire rack.

per 1/12 *recipe* *230 calories, 6 g fat (4 g sat fat), 4 g protein, 39 g carbohydrate, 16 mg cholesterol, 197 mg sodium*

GERMAN COFFEE CAKE

Yield: one 9-x-13-inch cake

There are many variations of German coffee cakes — this one uses sour cream in the topping.

DOUGH
3/4 cup milk
1 egg
3 tbs. butter or margarine
1 tsp. salt
2 tbs. sugar
3 cups all-purpose flour
1 1/2 tsp. rapid or quick yeast

TOPPING
1/2 cup sour cream
1/4 cup sugar
1 tsp. cinnamon

Remove dough from the machine upon completion of the dough cycle. Press into a lightly greased 9-x-13-inch baking pan, cover and let rise in a warm, draft-free location for 45 to 60 minutes, until almost to top of pan. After dough has risen, make small indentations in dough with your finger, randomly or in a pattern. Spread a thin layer of sour cream over dough — there will be slightly more sour cream in indentations. Mix sugar with cinnamon and sprinkle on top. Bake in a preheated 350° oven until bread is brown and crust is hard, about 25 to 30 minutes. Cool on a wire rack.

per 1/12 recipe   197 calories, 6 g fat (3 g sat fat), 5 g protein, 32 g carbohydrate, 30 mg cholesterol, 197 mg sodium

STREUSEL-TOPPED COFFEE CAKE

Yield: one 9-x-13-inch cake

*Similar to a **Moravian Coffee Cake**, this has a topping that can't be beat!*

DOUGH
1 cup milk
¼ cup butter or margarine
1 tsp. vanilla extract
¼ cup sugar
1 tsp. salt
3 cups all-purpose flour
1½ tsp. rapid or quick yeast
ADD: ½ cup chopped nuts of choice

TOPPING
½ cup all-purpose flour
¼ cup brown sugar, firmly packed
¼ cup sugar
1 tsp. cinnamon
¼ cup butter, cold, cut into small pieces

Add nuts to the machine after dough ball has formed, about 5 to 8 minutes after kneading starts. To make streusel topping, place all topping ingredients in a medium bowl. With your fingers or a pastry blender, rub or blend ingredients together until well mixed and crumbly; set aside.

Upon completion of the dough cycle, remove dough from machine and press into a lightly greased 9-x-13-inch baking pan. Make small indentations in dough with your finger, randomly or in a pattern. Press topping ingredients into indentations. Sprinkle any remaining topping over dough. Cover with a kitchen towel and place in a warm, draft-free location to rise for 45 to 60 minutes, or until almost to top of pan. Bake in a preheated 350° oven until bread is brown and crust is hard, about 25 to 30 minutes. Cool on a wire rack.

per $1/12$ *recipe*   *291 calories, 11 g fat (5 g sat fat), 5 g protein, 43 g carbohydrate, 21 mg cholesterol, 193 mg sodium*

SOUR CREAM COFFEE CAKE

Yield: one 9-x-13-inch cake

In this adaptation of a German coffee cake, the sour cream is in the dough. Although it is best eaten warm, any leftovers seem to disappear quickly.

DOUGH
1/4 cup milk
3/4 cup sour cream
2 tbs. butter or margarine
1 egg
1 tsp. vanilla extract
1/4 cup sugar
1 tsp. salt
3 cups all-purpose flour
2 tsp. rapid or quick yeast

TOPPING
1/2 cup all-purpose flour
1/4 cup brown sugar, firmly packed
1/4 cup sugar
1 tsp. cinnamon
1/2 cup butter, cold, cut into small pieces

To make streusel topping, place all topping ingredients in a medium bowl. With your fingers or a pastry blender, rub or blend ingredients together until well mixed and crumbly; set aside.

Upon completion of the dough cycle, remove dough from the machine and press into a greased 9-x-13-inch baking pan. Make small indentations in dough with your finger, randomly or in a pattern. Press topping ingredients into indentations, cover with a kitchen towel and place in a warm, draft-free location to rise for 45 to 60 minutes. Bake in a preheated 350° oven for 25 to 30 minutes. Cool on a wire rack.

per $1/_{12}$ **recipe**   *308 calories, 13 g fat (8 g sat fat), 5 g protein, 42 g carbohydrate, 50 mg cholesterol, 197 mg sodium*

BAGELS, ENGLISH MUFFINS AND DOUGHNUTS

DIRECTIONS FOR BAGELS . . 87
PLAIN BAGELS 88
EGG BAGELS 88
PUMPERNICKEL BAGELS . . 89
WHOLE WHEAT BAGELS . . 89
ONION BAGELS 90
ORANGE RAISIN BAGELS . . 90
CINNAMON RAISIN BAGELS . 91
APPLE CINNAMON RAISIN
   BAGELS 91
DIRECTIONS FOR ENGLISH
   MUFFINS 92
BASIC ENGLISH MUFFINS . . 92
WHOLE WHEAT ENGLISH
   MUFFINS 93
ORANGE RAISIN ENGLISH
   MUFFINS 93

CINNAMON RAISIN ENGLISH
   MUFFINS 94
ALMOND APRICOT ENGLISH
   MUFFINS 94
HAWAIIAN-STYLE ENGLISH
   MUFFINS 95
CRUMPETS 96
FRIED MEXICAN SWEET ROLLS
   (SOPAIPILLAS) 97
BASIC DOUGHNUTS 98
BEIGNETS 100
CHOCOLATE DOUGHNUTS . . 101
COCONUT DOUGHNUTS . . . 102
WEST INDIAN FLOATS . . . 103
FASTNACHTS 104

DIRECTIONS FOR BAGELS

Upon completion of the first kneading, turn off the machine and allow dough to sit undisturbed in the machine for about 45 minutes. Because bagels do not rise after shaping, preheat the oven to 450° and boil 2 quarts water in a large, nonaluminum pan before removing the dough from the machine. Once the water has come to a boil, stir in 1 tbs. sugar and lower the temperature so that the water maintains a steady, gentle boil.

Remove dough from the machine and form into 8 equal balls. Shape dough into bagels using any of the following methods:

- Roll each piece of dough into a rope and then shape into a circle, pressing the ends together. If dough does not seal, moisten dough lightly with a few drops of water.

- Roll each piece into a ball and slightly flatten between the heels of your palms. Push your thumb through the center to form a hole and twist dough to enlarge the hole.

- Remove dough from the machine and roll into a ½- to ¾-inch-thick rectangle on a lightly floured work surface. Cut bagels with a bagel or doughnut cutter.

Gently place 2 or 3 bagels at a time in the water. Cook the first side for 1½ to 2 minutes and then turn them over and cook the other side for another 1 to 1½ minutes (3 minutes total). Remove bagels with a slotted spoon and place on a well-greased perforated pizza pan (for crisp bottoms) or baking sheet.

Using a pastry brush, lightly brush bagels with beaten egg white and sprinkle with seeds if desired. Bake for 15 to 18 minutes or until golden brown.

PLAIN BAGELS

Yield: 8 bagels

Sprinkle with sesame, poppy, anise, fennel or caraway seeds, or instant onion flakes if desired.

1⅛ cups water
2 tbs. sugar
½ tsp. salt

3 cups all-purpose flour
2 tsp. rapid or quick yeast

Follow directions for making bagels on page 87.

per *⅛* ***recipe*** *184 calories, 0 g fat (0 g sat fat), 5 g protein, 39 g carbohydrate, 0 mg cholesterol, 136 mg sodium*

EGG BAGELS

Yield: 8 bagels

Sprinkle with poppy seeds if desired.

¾ cup water
2 eggs
2 tbs. sugar

½ tsp. salt
3 cups all-purpose flour
2 tsp. rapid or quick yeast

Follow directions for making bagels on page 87.

per *⅛* ***recipe*** *203 calories, 2 g fat (0 g sat fat), 7 g protein, 39 g carbohydrate, 53 mg cholesterol, 151 mg sodium*

PUMPERNICKEL BAGELS

Yield: 8 bagels

Sprinkle with caraway seeds as a finishing touch.

1¼ cups water
2 tbs. brown sugar
½ tsp. salt
1 tbs. unsweetened cocoa
½ cup rye flour

½ cup whole wheat flour
2 cups all-purpose flour
2 tsp. rapid or quick yeast
ADD: ⅓ cup raisins, optional

Follow directions for making bagels on page 87.

per ⅛ ***recipe*** *178 calories, 1 g fat (0 g sat fat), 5 g protein, 38 g carbohydrate, 0 mg cholesterol, 142 mg sodium*

WHOLE WHEAT BAGELS

Yield: 8 bagels

Sprinkle with sesame, poppy, anise, fennel or caraway seeds, or instant onion flakes if desired.

1⅛ cups water
2 tbs. brown sugar
½ tsp. salt

1 cup whole wheat flour
2 cups all-purpose flour
2 tsp. rapid or quick yeast

Follow directions for making bagels on page 87.

per ⅛ ***recipe*** *179 calories, 1 g fat (0 g sat fat), 6 g protein, 38 g carbohydrate, 0 mg cholesterol, 137 mg sodium*

ONION BAGELS

Yield: 8 bagels

Watch the dough; add water or flour a teaspoon at a time to obtain a smooth dough ball. Sprinkle with your favorite seeds or instant onion flakes if desired.

1⅛ cups water
¼ cup grated cheddar cheese, lightly
  packed
2 tbs. sugar

½ tsp. salt
2 tbs. instant onion flakes
3 cups all-purpose flour
2 tsp. rapid or quick yeast

Follow directions for making bagels on page 87.

per ⅛ recipe   201 calories, 2 g fat (1 g sat fat), 6 g protein, 40 g carbohydrate, 4 mg cholesterol, 158 mg sodium

ORANGE RAISIN BAGELS

Yield: 8 bagels

1¼ cups orange juice
2 tbs. sugar
½ tsp. salt
1 tsp. dried orange peel, or freshly
  grated to taste

3 cups all-purpose flour
2 tsp. rapid or quick yeast
ADD: ⅓ cup raisins, dried cranberries or
  other dried fruit

Follow directions for making bagels on page 87. Add raisins to the machine with dry ingredients at the beginning of the cycle.

per ⅛ recipe   223 calories, 1 g fat (0 g sat fat), 6 g protein, 49 g carbohydrate, 0 mg cholesterol, 136 mg sodium

CINNAMON RAISIN BAGELS

These are good sprinkled with poppy seeds.

1¼ cups water
2 tbs. sugar
½ tsp. salt
1 tsp. cinnamon, or to taste

3 cups all-purpose flour
2 tsp. rapid or quick yeast
ADD: ⅓ cup raisins or favorite dried fruit

Follow directions for making bagels on page 87. Add raisins to the machine with dry ingredients at the beginning of the cycle.

per ⅛ *recipe*   *206 calories, 1 g fat (0 g sat fat), 5 g protein, 45 g carbohydrate, 0 mg cholesterol, 137 mg sodium*

APPLE CINNAMON RAISIN BAGELS

1⅓ cups apple juice
2 tbs. sugar
½ tsp. salt
1 tsp. cinnamon, or to taste
½ cup oats

3 cups all-purpose flour
2 tsp. rapid or quick yeast
ADD: ¼ cup raisins
ADD: ¼ cup chopped dried apples

Follow directions for making bagels on page 87. Add raisins and dried apples to the machine with dry ingredients at the beginning of the cycle.

per ⅛ *recipe*   *244 calories, 1 g fat (0 g sat fat), 6 g protein, 53 g carbohydrate, 0 mg cholesterol, 138 mg sodium*

DIRECTIONS FOR ENGLISH MUFFINS

Remove dough from the machine upon completion of the dough cycle. Press dough by hand into a 1/2-inch-thick rectangle on a cornmeal-covered work surface. Turn dough over several times so that both sides are coated with cornmeal to prevent sticking. Cut muffins with a biscuit or cookie cutter, or use the top of a drinking glass. Place on a baking sheet, cover and let rise for 45 to 60 minutes.

Cook on an ungreased griddle (or cast-iron skillet) over low to medium heat for 5 to 7 minutes on each side or until golden. Cook muffins fairly close together — leave only about 1/2 inch between them. Split open with a fork and serve warm or toasted.

BASIC ENGLISH MUFFINS
Yield: 12-15 muffins

The softer the dough, the lighter the muffin will be.

1 cup milk
3 tbs. butter or margarine
1 egg
2 tsp. sugar

1/2 tsp. salt
3 cups all-purpose flour
1 1/2 tsp. rapid or quick yeast
ADD: cornmeal for rolling dough

Follow directions above.

per 1/12 recipe 158 calories, 4 g fat (2 g sat fat), 5 g protein, 26 g carbohydrate, 26 mg cholesterol, 106 mg sodium

WHOLE WHEAT ENGLISH MUFFINS

Yield: 12-15 muffins

Whole wheat adds a nutty flavor as well as nutrients.

1 cup milk
3 tbs. butter or margarine
1 egg
1 tbs. sugar
½ tsp. salt

1 cup whole wheat flour
2 cups all-purpose flour
1½ tsp. rapid or quick yeast
ADD: ½ cup raisins, optional
ADD: cornmeal for rolling dough

Follow directions on page 92. Add raisins 5 minutes after dough has formed a ball.

per ⅟₁₂ recipe   156 calories, 4 g fat (2 g sat fat), 5 g protein, 26 g carbohydrate, 26 mg cholesterol, 107 mg sodium

ORANGE RAISIN ENGLISH MUFFINS

Yield: 12-15 muffins

1 cup orange juice
2 tbs. butter or margarine
1 egg
¼-½ tsp. dried orange peel, or freshly
  grated to taste
2 tsp. sugar

½ tsp. salt
3-3¼ cups all-purpose flour
1½ tsp. rapid or quick yeast
ADD: ½ cup raisins or dried cranberries
ADD: cornmeal for rolling dough

Follow directions on page 92. Add raisins 5 minutes after dough has formed a ball.

per ⅟₁₂ recipe   173 calories, 3 g fat (1 g sat fat), 4 g protein, 33 g carbohydrate, 23 mg cholesterol, 96 mg sodium

CINNAMON RAISIN ENGLISH MUFFINS
Yield: 12-15 muffins

1 cup milk
3 tbs. butter or margarine
1 egg
1 tbs. sugar
1/2 tsp. salt

1 tsp. cinnamon, or to taste
3-3 1/4 cups all-purpose flour
1 1/2 tsp. rapid or quick yeast
ADD: 1/2 cup raisins
ADD: cornmeal for rolling dough

Follow directions on page 92. Add raisins 5 minutes after dough has formed a ball.

per 1/12 recipe   181 calories, 4 g fat (2 g sat fat), 5 g protein, 32 g carbohydrate, 26 mg cholesterol, 1077 mg sodium

ALMOND APRICOT ENGLISH MUFFINS
Yield: 12-15 muffins

1 cup orange juice
1 egg
2 tbs. butter or margarine
2 tsp. almond extract
1 tbs. sugar
1/2 tsp. salt

3-3 1/4 cups all-purpose flour
1 1/2 tsp. rapid or quick yeast
ADD: 1/4 cup finely diced apricots
ADD: 1/4 cup finely chopped almonds
ADD: cornmeal for rolling dough

Follow directions on page 92. Add apricots and nuts 5 minutes after dough has formed a ball.

per 1/12 recipe   173 calories, 4 g fat (2 g sat fat), 5 g protein, 29 g carbohydrate, 23 mg cholesterol, 97 mg sodium

HAWAIIAN-STYLE ENGLISH MUFFINS

These muffins are really special. The recipe calls for macadamia nuts for a tropical flavor, but almonds could be used as a less expensive alternative.

1 cup pineapple juice
2 tbs. butter or margarine
1 egg
2 tsp. coconut extract
1 tbs. sugar
1/2 tsp. salt
1/2 cup coconut flakes
3 cups all-purpose flour
1 1/2 tsp. rapid or quick yeast
ADD: 1/4 cup finely chopped macadamia nuts
ADD: cornmeal for rolling dough

Follow directions on page 92. Add macadamia nuts about 5 minutes after dough has formed a ball.

per 1/12 *recipe* 190 calories, 6 g fat (3 g sat fat), 4 g protein, 30 g carbohydrate, 23 mg cholesterol, 104 mg sodium

CRUMPETS

The dough for crumpets is really more like a batter and will have to be poured into crumpet rings on a hot griddle or (cast iron) frying pan. Do not make this recipe in a Welbilt, DAK or Citizen machine because of the hole in the bottom of the pan. Crumpets are best eaten warm or toasted, with lots of butter.

1¼ cups milk
2 tbs. butter
1 egg
1 tbs. sugar

1 tsp. salt
2 cups all-purpose flour
2 tsp. rapid or quick yeast

Use the dough cycle to knead batter. Once the machine has completed kneading, allow dough (batter) to rise for 45 to 50 minutes. About 30 minutes into the rising phase, start preheating a cast-iron skillet or griddle over low heat. Lightly grease crumpet rings (you can use clean, empty tuna fish cans or similar cans with both ends removed). Place ring(s) on the griddle and spoon about 2 tbs. batter into each ring. Cook batter for about 3 minutes until it is bubbly, firm and lightly browned on the bottom. Slide a spatula underneath ring to pick up ring and crumpet. Remove hot ring and cook second side of crumpet until it is lightly browned on the bottom. Repeat the process until batter is used.

per 1/24 **recipe** *57 calories, 2 g fat (1 g sat fat), 2 g protein, 9 g carbohydrate, 12 mg cholesterol, 98 mg sodium*

FRIED MEXICAN SWEET ROLLS (SOPAIPILLAS)

This favorite Mexican sweet roll may be enjoyed with a meal or for dessert. Sprinkle with cinnamon sugar or confectioners' sugar or eat with honey. The softer the dough, the lighter the sopaipilla, so take care when adding flour.

1 cup milk
2 tbs. butter
1 egg
2 tbs. sugar

1 tsp. salt
3-3¼ cups all-purpose flour
2 tsp. rapid or quick yeast
oil for deep frying

Remove dough from the machine upon completion of the dough cycle. Roll dough into large rectangle on a lightly floured work surface to prevent sticking. Fold dough in half and roll out into another large rectangle. With a sharp knife or a pizza wheel, cut dough into small rectangles and then in half to make 2 triangles (or other desired shape). Fry 2 at a time for 1 to 2 minutes on each side in a full (4-cup) deep fat fryer. They should puff up and are done when lightly golden in color.

*per ¹⁄₁₂ **recipe without fat for frying*** *146 calories, 3 g fat (1 g sat fat), 5 g protein, 25 g carbohydrate, 23 mg cholesterol, 195 mg sodium*

BASIC DOUGHNUTS

Yield: 12-15 doughnuts

This dough is made the evening before and rises in the refrigerator overnight. The dough should be slightly sticky. The overnight refrigeration accomplishes two things. First, the cold rising makes the sticky dough easier to roll and handle. Second, it allows you to have fresh doughnuts early in the morning! With the exception of Welbilt, DAK and Citizen machines (because of the hole in the bottom of the pan), the dough may be loosely covered with plastic wrap right in the bread machine pan and placed in the refrigerator. Otherwise, place the dough in a lightly greased glass or plastic bowl, cover with plastic wrap and refrigerate. Oh, yes — and don't forget to fry the "holes"!

1 cup milk
2 tbs. butter or margarine
1 egg
½ cup sugar
1 tsp. salt
3 cups all-purpose flour
1½ tsp. rapid or quick yeast
oil for deep frying

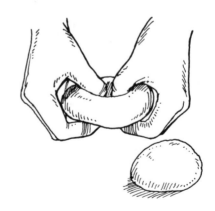

Upon completion of the kneading (before the rising phase), remove the pan containing dough, cover lightly with plastic wrap and place in the refrigerator to rise overnight. In the morning, remove dough, place on a lightly floured work surface and roll into a ½-inch thickness. The softer the dough, the lighter the doughnut, so take care when adding flour. It may be helpful to grease your hands when handling dough to prevent sticking. Cut doughnut shapes with a greased or floured doughnut cutter and place on a well-greased baking sheet. Cover with a kitchen towel and let rise until light and airy (1 to 1½ hours). Fry 2 at a time in a full (4-cup) deep fat fryer.

TIP: If you don't have a doughnut cutter, use a cookie cutter. Tear out a hole with your fingers.

per ¹⁄₁₂ ***recipe without fat for frying*** *177 calories, 3 g fat (1 g sat fat), 5 g protein, 33 g carbohydrate, 23 mg cholesterol, 195 mg sodium*

BEIGNETS

No visit to New Orleans would be complete without enjoying these for breakfast. This dough is made the evening before and rises in the refrigerator overnight. Cover the dough in the machine pan loosely with plastic wrap and refrigerate. If you have a Welbilt, DAK or Citizen machine (with a hole in the bottom of the pan), place the dough in a lightly greased glass or plastic bowl, cover with plastic wrap and refrigerate. Serve with confectioners' or cinnamon sugar. Do not add too much flour.

⅞ cup (7 oz.) milk
2 tbs. butter
1 egg
¼ cup sugar
1 tsp. salt

1 tsp. cinnamon, optional
3 cups all-purpose flour
1½ tsp. rapid or quick yeast
oil for deep frying

Upon completion of the kneading, cover dough lightly with plastic wrap and place in the refrigerator to rise overnight. In the morning, remove dough, place on a lightly floured work surface and roll into a ½-inch thickness. With a sharp knife or pizza wheel, cut dough into 2- or 3-inch squares and place on a well-greased baking sheet. Cover with a kitchen towel and let rise for about 1 hour. Fry 2 at a time in a full (4-cup) deep fat fryer.

per ¹⁄₁₂ recipe without fat for frying *163 calories, 3 g fat (1 g sat fat), 5 g protein, 29 g carbohydrate, 23 mg cholesterol, 193 mg sodium*

CHOCOLATE DOUGHNUTS

Yield: 12-15 doughnuts

*If you like the combination of chocolate and coconut as much as I do, try glazing these doughnuts with **Coconut Glaze**, page 159.*

1 cup milk
2 tbs. butter or margarine
1 egg
½ cup sugar
1 tsp. salt

2 tbs. unsweetened cocoa
3 cups all-purpose flour
1½ tsp. rapid or quick yeast
oil for deep frying

Upon completion of the kneading, remove dough, cover lightly with plastic wrap and place in the refrigerator to rise overnight. In the morning, remove dough, place on a lightly floured work surface and roll into a ½-inch thickness. The softer the dough, the lighter the doughnut, so take care when adding flour. It may be helpful to grease your hands when handling dough to prevent sticking. Cut doughnut shapes with a greased or floured doughnut cutter and place on a well-greased baking sheet. Cover with a kitchen towel and let rise until light and airy (1 to 1½ hours). Fry 2 at a time in a full (4-cup) deep fat fryer.

*per ¹⁄₁₂ **recipe without fat for frying*** *180 calories, 3 g fat (1 g sat fat), 5 g protein, 34 g carbohydrate, 23 mg cholesterol, 201 mg sodium*

COCONUT DOUGHNUTS

Yield: 12-15 doughnuts

You'll think you're in the tropics when you eat these breakfast doughnuts! The softer the dough, the lighter the doughnut, so take care when adding flour. It may be helpful to grease your hands when handling the dough to prevent sticking.

1¼ cups canned, unsweetened
  coconut milk
2 tbs. butter or margarine
1 egg
¼ cup sugar

1 tsp. salt
½ cup coconut flakes
3 cups all-purpose flour
1½ tsp. rapid or quick yeast
oil for deep frying

Upon completion of the kneading, remove dough, cover lightly with plastic wrap and place in the refrigerator to rise overnight. In the morning, remove dough, place on a lightly floured work surface and roll into a ½-inch thickness. Cut doughnut shapes with a greased or floured doughnut cutter and place on a well-greased baking sheet. Cover with a kitchen towel and let rise until light and airy (1 to 1½ hours). Fry 2 at a time in a full (4-cup) deep fat fryer.

per ¹/₁₂ recipe without fat for frying *215 calories, 9 g fat (7 g sat fat), 4 g protein, 30 g carbohydrate, 23 mg cholesterol, 195 mg sodium*

WEST INDIAN FLOATS

Yield: 12 fried breads

These fried breads are usually served with fish, but may also be eaten alone any time of the day. Unlike many of the other fried breads, these are not sweet.

1 cup water
2 tbs. shortening or butter
1 tsp. salt
3 cups all-purpose flour
1½ tsp. rapid or quick yeast
oil for frying

Remove dough from the machine upon completion of the dough cycle. Divide dough into 12 equal pieces and shape into balls. Place on a greased baking sheet, cover and let rise for about 30 minutes. Fry for about 2 minutes on each side in a full (4-cup) deep fat fryer or in a few inches of vegetable oil until golden brown.

per ¹⁄₁₂ *recipe without fat for frying* 134 calories, 2 g fat (1 g sat fat), 3 g protein, 24 g carbohydrate, 0 mg cholesterol, 179 mg sodium

BAGELS, ENGLISH MUFFINS AND DOUGHNUTS   103

FASTNACHTS

These German "doughnuts" are eaten just before Lent and the name means, literally, "night before fasting." They are enjoyed by the Pennsylvania Dutch as well. While they may be eaten just as they are, we like to sprinkle them with confectioners' sugar or cinnamon sugar. The softer the dough, the lighter the results, so take care when adding flour.

1 cup milk
2 tbs. butter
1 egg
1 tsp. vanilla extract
1/4 cup sugar
1 tsp. salt

1 tsp. dried lemon peel, or freshly
  grated to taste
1/2 cup instant potato flakes
3 cups all-purpose flour
1 1/2 tsp. rapid or quick yeast
oil for deep frying

Upon completion of the dough cycle, remove dough, place on a lightly floured work surface and roll into a 1/2-inch thickness. With a sharp knife or pizza wheel, cut dough into 2- or 3-inch diamond shapes and place on a well-greased baking sheet. Cover with a kitchen towel and let rise for about 30 minutes. Fry 2 at a time in a full (4-cup) deep fat fryer.

per 1/12 **recipe without oil for frying** *169 calories, 3 g fat (1 g sat fat), 5 g protein, 31 g carbohydrate, 23 mg cholesterol, 197 mg sodium*

ETHNIC BREADS

CRUSTY MEXICAN ROLLS
  (BOLILLOS AND TELERAS) . . . 106
GREEK PSOMI 108
FRENCH FLATBREAD
  (FOUGASSE) 110
PITA BREAD 111
PERSIAN FLATBREAD
  (BARBARI) 112
INDIAN FLATBREAD (NAAN) . . 113
KAISER ROLLS 114
MIDDLE EASTERN SESAME
  RINGS (SIMIT) 115
MEXICAN SWEET ROLLS
  (PAN DULCE) 116
ARMENIAN ROLLS 118
MAHLAB RINGS 119

ROSEMARY RAISIN BREAD . 120
ANISE SESAME ROLLS . . . 121
MEDITERRANEAN CHEESE
  FLATBREADS 122
FRENCH WALNUT ROLLS . . 124
GOLDEN VALENCIAN ROLLS . 125
SPANISH SUGAR ROLLS . . 126
KUGELHOPF 127
CROISSANTS 128
SCOTTISH ROWIES 130
GERMAN FARM BREAD . . . 132
MIDDLE EASTERN FLATBREAD
  (CHUREK) 134
CHALLAH 135
BUTTERFLAKE ROUNDS . . 136
CHINESE STEAMED BUNS . . 137

Many of the breads in this chapter require a steam treatment to achieve a crisp, crusty exterior. Refer to pages 14 and 15 for steaming methods.

CRUSTY MEXICAN ROLLS (BOLILLOS AND TELERAS)

Yield: 12 rolls

These two crusty Mexican rolls are made from the same basic dough, but are shaped differently. The flavor develops while the sponge sits overnight or during the day. Mr. and Mrs. Polk say that they make these rolls all the time in their machine. Use your favorite method(s) for generating steam for a crisp crust (see pages 14-15).

SPONGE*
1/3 cup water
1 tsp. sugar
1/4 tsp. salt
3/4 cup all-purpose flour
1 tsp. rapid or quick yeast

DOUGH
*sponge
3/4 cup water
1 tsp. sugar
1 tsp. salt
2 cups all-purpose flour

1 tsp. rapid or quick yeast
1-2 tbs. water if necessary

Add sponge ingredients to the machine pan, start the machine and allow it to knead sponge for 5 to 10 minutes. Turn off machine and allow sponge to sit undisturbed in the pan for 6 to 10 hours. If you have a Welbilt, DAK or Citizen machine or if your machine is otherwise occupied, mix sponge in a large bowl, cover with plastic wrap and allow to sit undisturbed in a warm, draft-free location for 6 to 10 hours.

After 6 to 10 hours, add remaining dough ingredients, except water, to sponge and start the dough cycle. Allow dough to knead for a few minutes and then add 1 to 2 tbs. water to soften dough if necessary. Upon completion of dough cycle, remove dough from machine and roll it into a long rope about 2 inches thick. Divide dough into 12 equal pieces and flatten each into an oval between your hands.

For bolillos: Fold one third (lengthwise) of the oval over towards the center and flatten with your hands. Fold the other third over on top of the previous fold and flatten it again with your hands. Roll dough slightly to tighten; round the ends. Place dough seam side up on greased baking sheets.

For teleras: With a small rolling pin or the handle of a wooden spoon, press down in the center of the oval (lengthwise) so that dough is almost cut in half. Turn each piece upside down and place on a greased baking sheet.

Cover bolillos and/or teleras with a towel and place in a warm, draft-free location for 1 hour. Bake in a preheated 400° oven until golden brown, about 15 to 20 minutes.

per 1/12 *recipe*   *108 calories, 0 g fat (0 g sat fat), 3 g protein, 23 g carbohydrate, 0 mg cholesterol, 420 mg sodium*

GREEK PSOMI

Who can resist this light and airy bread with a crisp crust? The folding technique helps to give it the light texture.

DOUGH
1 cup water
1 tbs. olive oil
2 tbs. honey
1 tsp. salt
3 cups bread flour
1½ tsp. rapid or quick yeast

WASH
cold water

Remove dough from the machine upon completion of the dough cycle. Roll into a long rope about 2 inches thick. Divide dough into 4 equal pieces and flatten each one into an oval between your hands. Fold one third (lengthwise) of the dough towards the center and flatten with your hands. Fold the other third on top of the previous fold and flatten it again with your hands. Roll dough slightly to tighten; round the ends. Place dough seam side up on greased baking sheets. Cover and let rise in a warm, draft-free location for 45 minutes to 1 hour. While bread is rising, preheat oven to 400°. About 5 minutes before putting bread in oven, place a shallow pan with 1 or 2 inches of water on bottom shelf of oven or use another method to obtain a crisp crust (see pages 14-15). Slash top of each mini-loaf with a sharp knife or razor blade, spray or wash with cold water and bake for 10 to 15 minutes.

per $\frac{1}{12}$ ***recipe***   *122 calories, 2 g fat (0 g sat fat), 4 g protein, 23 g carbohydrate, 0 mg cholesterol, 179 mg sodium*

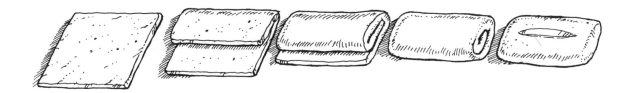

FRENCH FLATBREAD (FOUGASSE)

This crusty flatbread is enjoyed in Southern France. Use your favorite method to obtain a crisp crust (see pages 14-15).

DOUGH
1 cup water
2 tbs. olive oil
1 tsp. salt
3 cups bread flour
1½ tsp. rapid or quick yeast

WASH
cold water

Remove dough from the machine upon completion of the dough cycle. Divide dough into 6 equal pieces and let rest for about 10 minutes. Roll each piece into an oval or triangle and place on a lightly greased baking sheet. Cover with a towel and let rise in a warm, draft-free location for 45 minutes to 1 hour. While bread is rising, preheat oven to 400°. About 5 minutes before putting bread in oven, place a shallow pan with 1 or 2 inches of water on bottom shelf of oven. With your fingertips, press several indentations into dough and then slash an X into top with a very sharp knife or a razor blade. Spray or brush with cold water. Bake for 10 to 12 minutes or until golden.

per ⅙ recipe 242 calories, 6 g fat (0 g sat fat), 7 g protein, 41 g carbohydrate, 0 mg cholesterol, 357 mg sodium

PITA BREAD

The secrets to getting pitas to puff are a very hot oven and a preheated baking sheet, pizza stone or pizza tiles. Let the pitas rise on a flat, cornmeal-covered surface (a rimless baking sheet or pizza peel) and slide them onto the heated pan or stone. If for some reason the pitas don't puff, wrap them around your filling.

DOUGH
1¼ cups water
3 tbs. olive oil
2 tbs. sugar

1 tsp. salt
3 cups bread flour
2 tsp. rapid or quick yeast

WASH
olive oil, optional

Remove dough from the machine upon completion of the dough cycle. Form dough into 8 equal balls and flatten each ball into a round with a rolling pin or your hands. Place on a cornmeal-covered pizza peel or other flat surface, cover with a towel and let rise in a warm, draft-free location for 20 to 30 minutes. Brush with olive oil, if desired. Slide pita rounds onto a preheated baking sheet or pizza stone in a preheated 500° oven for 8 to 12 minutes.

per ⅛ **recipe**   *208 calories, 6 g fat (1 g sat fat), 5 g protein, 34 g carbohydrate, 0 mg cholesterol, 268 mg sodium*

PERSIAN FLATBREAD (BARBARI)

Yield: 4 flatbreads

These traditional Iranian breads are used to scoop up foods or to soak up sauces. Unlike pita breads, these are scored to prevent pockets from forming. Various seeds (sesame, anise or fennel) may be sprinkled onto the dough just before baking.

DOUGH
1 cup water
2 tbs. olive oil
1 tsp. salt
3 cups all-purpose flour
2 tsp. rapid or quick yeast

WASH
olive oil

TOPPING
sesame, anise or fennel seeds, optional

Remove dough from the machine upon completion of the dough cycle and form into 4 equal balls. Brush each ball lightly with olive oil and roll or press each into a round or rectangle. Brush with additional oil if necessary to prevent sticking. Place on a lightly greased baking sheet, cover and let rise for 20 to 30 minutes. Brush tops with more olive oil. With a sharp knife or razor blade, score 4 or 5 parallel lines across the length and width of bread so that bread is covered with little squares. Top with seeds, if desired. Bake in a preheated 425° oven for 12 to 15 minutes.

***per** 1/4 **recipe**   363 calories, 8 g fat (1 g sat fat), 11 g protein, 61 g carbohydrate, 0 mg cholesterol, 535 mg sodium*

INDIAN FLATBREAD (NAAN)

Yield: 8 flatbreads

Indian naan may be leavened either with yeast or baking powder. If leavened with baking powder, they are traditionally baked on the walls of a tandoor oven. Either way, yogurt is a main ingredient in the bread. Start with 1/4 cup water and use more if you need it to make the dough into a round, smooth ball.

1/2 cup yogurt
1/4-1/2 cup water
2 tbs. vegetable oil
1 1/2 tsp. sugar
1 tsp. salt
3 cups all-purpose flour
2 tsp. rapid or quick yeast

Remove dough from the machine upon completion of the dough cycle and divide into 8 equal pieces. Roll each piece into a small round, place on a lightly greased baking sheet and immediately bake in a preheated 500° oven for 5 to 7 minutes.

per 1/8 recipe   213 calories, 4 g fat (1 g sat fat), 6 g protein, 38 g carbohydrate, 1 mg cholesterol, 279 mg sodium

KAISER ROLLS

These rolls are famous for a crisp crust (from baking in steam, see pages 14-15) and light, airy interior. The dough is very soft, but the texture will be dramatically affected if too much flour is added, so use nonstick vegetable spray to handle dough.

DOUGH
1¼ cups water
1 tbs. vegetable oil
1 tbs. sugar
1 tsp. salt
3 cups bread flour
2 tsp. rapid or quick yeast

WASH
ice water

TOPPING
sesame seeds

Remove dough from the machine upon completion of the dough cycle and divide into 8 equal pieces. On a greased work surface, roll each piece into a 6- or 7-inch round. Fold one edge to the middle. Starting about halfway along that fold, fold another piece to the middle. When you get around to the first fold, you should have 5 folds (see page 9). Tuck the last half of the last fold under the first fold, press firmly to seal and place folded side up on a greased baking sheet. Cover and let rise for about 1 hour. Brush or spray with ice water and sprinkle with seeds. Bake in a preheated 450° oven for 12 to 15 minutes.

per ⅛ recipe   *173 calories, 2 g fat (4.4 g sat fat), 5 g protein, 32 g carbohydrate, 0 mg cholesterol, 268 mg sodium*

MIDDLE EASTERN
SESAME RINGS (SIMIT)

Yield: 12 rings

Simit rings are sold by street venders in many parts of the Middle East. Sesame seeds are purchased less expensively in bulk at health food stores or by mail order.

DOUGH
1 cup water
2 tbs. vegetable or olive oil
2 tbs. sugar
1 tsp. salt
3 cups all-purpose flour
1½ tsp. rapid or quick yeast

WASH
1 egg beaten with 1-2 tbs. water

TOPPING
2-3 cups sesame seeds

Remove dough from the machine upon completion of the dough cycle. Divide dough into 12 equal pieces. Roll each piece into a long roll and pinch ends together to form a ring. Brush dough liberally with egg wash and then dip rounds into a plate of sesame seeds to coat. Use lots of seeds! Place seeded rounds on a greased baking sheet, cover and let rise in a warm, draft-free location for about 30 minutes. Bake in a preheated 400° oven for 15 to 20 minutes or until golden brown (the longer they bake, the crisper they are).

per 1/12 *recipe* 280 calories, 15 g fat (2 g sat fat), 8 g protein, 32 g carbohydrate, 0 mg cholesterol, 182 mg sodium

ETHNIC BREADS   115

MEXICAN SWEET ROLLS (PAN DULCE)

Yield: 8 rolls

Raymond Johnson says that he and his wife, Patty, enjoy making these sweet Mexican rolls with this special topping. They used to buy them at a local bakery but Raymond adapted a recipe for his machine and they now make them at home.

DOUGH
⅝ cup (5 oz.) milk
2 tbs. butter
1 egg
1 tsp. vanilla extract
3 tbs. sugar
½ tsp. salt
2 cups bread flour
1½ tsp. yeast

TOPPING
¾ cup all-purpose flour
¾ cup confectioners' sugar
¼ cup butter, cut into several pieces
1 egg yolk
1 tbs. vanilla extract

For topping, mix together flour and sugar. With your fingers or a pastry blender, cut in cold butter until a granular (cornmeal) consistency is obtained. Add egg yolk and vanilla. Mix into a stiff dough. Divide mixture into 8 equal pieces, flatten into small rounds (about 3 inches) and place on a sheet of waxed paper; set aside.

Grease your hands to remove dough upon completion of the dough cycle. Divide dough into 8 equal pieces and flatten each between your hands into small 3-inch rounds. Place each round on a lightly greased baking sheet. Place a piece of topping on each round. With a sharp knife or razor blade, score a line or two in the topping. Cover with a towel and place in a warm, draft-free location to rise for about 30 minutes. Bake in a preheated 350° oven for about 15 minutes.

per ⅛ *recipe*   *301 calories, 11 g fat (6 g sat fat), 7 g protein, 44 g carbohydrate, 77 mg cholesterol, 156 mg sodium*

ARMENIAN ROLLS

These delicious coffee rolls are based on an Armenian recipe that uses sesame seed paste (tahini) instead of peanut butter. Use tahini if you have it.

DOUGH
3/4 cup milk
1/4 cup butter or margarine
1 egg
2 tbs. sugar
1/2 tsp. salt
3 1/2 cups all-purpose flour
1 1/2 tsp. rapid or quick yeast

FILLING
1/3-1/2 cup peanut butter
3-4 tbs. brown sugar

WASH
1 egg beaten with 1 scant tbs. milk

Upon completion of the dough cycle, divide dough into 8 equal pieces and roll into small 6- to 8-inch rectangles. Spread each one with a large spoonful of peanut butter and sprinkle with about 1 tsp. brown sugar. Roll each rectangle jelly-roll fashion, beginning on the wide side (see page 9), and pull into a long, twisted rope. Coil each rope (see page 6) and tuck the end underneath. Place on a greased baking sheet, cover and let rise in a warm, draft-free location for about 30 minutes. Brush tops with egg wash and bake in a preheated 350° oven for 15 to 20 minutes.

per 1/8 recipe 363 calories, 12 g fat (5 g sat fat), 10 g protein, 54 g carbohydrate, 42 mg cholesterol, 159 mg sodium

MAHLAB RINGS

*This is a yeasted adaptation of a Middle Eastern pastry ring. Mahlab, from black cherry seeds, must be crushed with a mortar and pestle. See **Sources**, page 165.*

DOUGH
3/4 cup milk
2 tbs. corn or vegetable oil
1 egg
2 tbs. sugar
1 tsp. salt
1 tsp. ground mahlab or allspice
3 cups all-purpose flour
1 1/2 tsp. rapid or quick yeast

FILLING
2 tbs. lemon juice
2 tbs. sugar
1/3-1/2 cup sesame seeds

Upon completion of the dough cycle, remove dough from the machine and roll into a large rectangle. Mix together lemon juice and sugar; coat dough with lemon mixture with a brush. Sprinkle with sesame seeds. Cut dough into small rectangles 6 inches x 1/2 inch. Twist each rectangle into a long spiral and curl into a ring, pinching ends closed to seal. Place twisted rings on a lightly greased baking sheet, cover with a towel and place in a warm, draft-free location to rise for about 1 hour. Bake in a preheated 350° oven for 20 to 25 minutes or until lightly browned.

per 1/12 **recipe**   *186 calories, 5 g fat (1 g sat fat), 5 g protein, 30 g carbohydrate, 18 mg cholesterol, 193 mg sodium*

ROSEMARY RAISIN BREAD

Yield: 4 rounds

This Italian bread is unique because the raisins are first sautéed in olive oil. The mashed raisins will impart flavor throughout the loaf. Use fresh rosemary if you can.

DOUGH

2 tbs. golden raisins sautéed in
  1 tbs. olive oil
1 cup water
1 tbs. honey
1 tsp. salt
1 tbs. chopped fresh rosemary, or 1 tsp. dried
3 cups bread flour
2 tsp. rapid or quick yeast

WASH
cold water

Remove raisins from heat and cool to lukewarm. Add raisins and olive oil to the bread machine with other liquid ingredients. Upon completion of the dough cycle, divide dough into 4 equal pieces. With your hands, flatten each piece into a 1-inch-thick round and place on a greased baking sheet. Cover and let rise in a warm, draft-free location for 20 to 30 minutes. Just before baking, slash an X in top of each round, wash or spray with cold water and bake in a preheated 350° oven for about 30 minutes or until golden brown.

per ¼ recipe   *366 calories, 5 g fat (1 g sat fat), 11 g protein, 70 g carbohydrate, 0 mg cholesterol, 536 mg sodium*

ANISE SESAME ROLLS

Yield: 8-10 rolls

Not only is the combination of anise and sesame seeds a favorite in the Mediterranean countries and Middle East, but it is in Mexico too! Crush the anise seeds lightly with a mortar and pestle or between two spoons to bring out their flavor.

DOUGH
¾ cup milk
2 tbs. butter or margarine
1 egg
¼ cup sugar
1 tsp. salt
1 tsp. anise seed, lightly crushed
3 cups all-purpose flour
1½ tsp. rapid or quick yeast

WASH
1 egg white beaten with 1 tbs. water

TOPPING
sesame seeds

Upon completion of the dough cycle, remove dough from the machine and divide into 8 to 10 equal pieces. Place on a lightly greased baking sheet, cover and let rise for about 1 hour. With a sharp knife or razor blade, slash an X in the top of each roll. Brush with egg wash and liberally sprinkle with sesame seeds. Bake in a 350° oven for 15 to 20 minutes or until golden brown.

per ¹⁄₁₀ *recipe   244 calories, 8 g fat (2 g sat fat), 7 g protein, 37 g carbohydrate, 28 mg cholesterol, 231 mg sodium*

MEDITERRANEAN CHEESE FLATBREADS

Yield: 6 rounds

If you are looking for a special bread to accompany an Italian-flavored meal, use mozzarella cheese. I use feta with a lamb dinner or a Greek salad. Pine nuts are the favored, traditional nut, but walnuts make an easy, less expensive substitution.

DOUGH
1 cup water
2 tbs. olive oil
2 oz. (½ cup) grated mozzarella or
  feta cheese
1 tbs. chopped fresh basil, or 1 tsp. dried
1 tbs. sugar
1 tsp. salt
¼ cup ground pine nuts or walnuts
3 cups bread flour
1½ tsp. rapid or quick yeast

WASH
olive oil

Add ground pine nuts or walnuts to the machine 5 minutes after machine starts kneading, regardless of the type of machine. Upon completion of the dough cycle, remove dough and divide into 6 equal pieces. Roll each piece into a round and place on a lightly greased baking sheet. Cover with a towel and let rise in a warm, draft-free location for 45 minutes to 1 hour. With your fingertips, press several indentations into dough and then brush with olive oil. Bake in a preheated 500° oven for 5 to 8 minutes or until golden.

per ⅙ **recipe**   *325 calories, 12 g fat (3 g sat fat), 11 g protein, 45 g carbohydrate, 8 mg cholesterol, 463 mg sodium*

FRENCH WALNUT ROLLS

Yield: 6 rolls

These rustic French country breads are often served with nothing more than cheese. The walnuts add both flavor and color. Walnut oil, available in large grocery stores, imparts additional flavor. Vegetable oil may be substituted.

DOUGH
1 cup water
1 tbs. walnut or vegetable oil
1 tsp. sugar
1/2 tsp. salt

3 cups bread flour
1 1/2 tsp. rapid or quick yeast
ADD: 1/4-1/3 cup chopped walnuts

WASH
cold water

Add walnuts to dough about 5 minutes after dough ball has formed. Upon completion of the dough cycle, remove dough from the machine, divide into 6 equal pieces and shape into balls. Place on a greased baking sheet, cover and let rise for 45 minutes to 1 hour. With a sharp razor blade or knife, cut an X or a tic-tac-toe pattern on top of each roll, brush or spray with cold water and bake in a preheated 350° oven until rolls are brown and sound hollow when tapped, about 15 to 20 minutes.

*per 1/6 **recipe** 256 calories, 6 g fat (1 g sat fat), 9 g protein, 42 g carbohydrate, 0 mg cholesterol, 180 mg sodium*

GOLDEN VALENCIAN ROLLS

Yield: 8 rolls

The beaten egg white makes a meringue-like topping. The dough and the rolls are very heavy and dense in nature. Scrape the sides of the pan with a rubber spatula if necessary to help form a dough ball — and add a tiny bit of milk to soften the dough if the machine seems to struggle.

DOUGH
⅔ cup milk
⅓ cup vegetable oil
2 eggs
½ cup sugar
1 tsp. salt
4 cups all-purpose flour
2 tsp. rapid or quick yeast

TOPPING
1 egg white beaten until stiff

ADDITIONAL INGREDIENT
sugar

Remove dough from the machine upon completion of the dough cycle. Divide dough into 8 equal pieces and shape each into a ball. Place on a greased baking sheet, cover and let rise in a warm, draft-free location for about 2 hours. After rising, gently spread 1 tsp. stiffly beaten egg white onto each ball. Sprinkle each with a pinch of sugar and bake in a preheated 350° oven for 30 to 35 minutes or until the bread is a deep golden color.

per ⅛ recipe   386 calories, 11 g fat (1 g sat fat), 9 g protein, 62 g carbohydrate, 54 mg cholesterol, 301 mg sodium

SPANISH SUGAR ROLLS

The secret to these sweet rolls is filling the slashed top with sugar. A few drops of yellow food coloring may be added to the dough for a richer color if desired.

DOUGH
7/8 cup (7 oz.) water
2 tbs. butter or margarine
1 egg
1/4 cup sugar
1/2 tsp. salt
3 cups all-purpose flour
2 tsp. rapid or quick yeast

ADDITIONAL INGREDIENT
2 tbs. sugar

WASH
1 whole egg beaten with 2 tbs. milk

Remove dough from the machine upon completion of the dough cycle. Form dough into 12 equal balls or ovals. With a very sharp knife or razor blade, make a deep slash going about halfway through the middle of each ball. Place on a greased baking sheet, cover and let rise in a warm, draft-free location for about 1 hour. After rising, fill each slashed opening with 1/2 tsp. sugar. Brush tops of rolls with egg wash, avoiding sugared slashes, and bake in a preheated 350° oven for 15 to 20 minutes or until golden.

*per 1/12 **recipe** 151 calories, 2 g fat (1 g sat fat), 4 g protein, 28 g carbohydrate, 18 mg cholesterol, 119 mg sodium*

KUGELHOPF

Yield: 1 loaf

Serve this with fruit preserves for a festive treat. Special kugelhopf molds are available by mail order catalog or at kitchen specialty shops. I use a Bundt pan.

DOUGH

¾ cup milk
2 tbs. butter or margarine
3 eggs
½ cup sugar
1 tsp. salt

3½ cups all-purpose flour
2 tsp. rapid or quick yeast
ADD: ½ cup golden raisins or chopped
    favorite dried fruit (or combination)
ADD: ¼ cup chopped or sliced almonds

ADDITIONAL INGREDIENTS

¼ cup coarsely chopped or sliced almonds
confectioners' sugar

Add raisins and ¼ cup almonds to the machine about 5 minutes after the dough ball has been formed. Heavily grease a Bundt pan or kugelhopf mold and sprinkle additional ¼ cup almonds on the bottom. Upon completion of the dough cycle, scrape dough into prepared pan. Cover with a kitchen towel and let rise for 1½ to 2 hours in a warm, draft-free location. Bake in a preheated 350° oven for about 30 minutes until nicely browned. Cool on a wire rack. Dust with confectioners' sugar.

*per ¹⁄₁₂ **recipe** 260 calories, 6 g fat (2 g sat fat), 7 g protein, 44 g carbohydrate, 58 mg cholesterol, 204 mg sodium*

CROISSANTS

Yield: about 12 medium croissants

The key to flaky, light croissants is folding butter into the dough repeatedly. The soft dough is easier to work if it has been refrigerated before each folding. Making croissants is not a difficult process, but it is somewhat time-consuming because of the need to work the dough every half hour or so. If at any time the dough becomes too sticky or the butter starts to break through, place it in the refrigerator for 10 to 15 minutes. The dough is a bit on the wet side, which contributes to the lightness of the final product, so add flour only if necessary. Croissants may be frozen and then heated in a medium (350° to 375°) oven for about 5 minutes.

DOUGH

1¼ cups milk
1 tbs. sugar
½ tsp. salt
3 cups all-purpose flour
2 tsp. rapid or quick yeast

ADDITIONAL INGREDIENTS

¾ cup butter, softened
1 tbs. butter, melted

Remove dough pan with dough from the machine upon completion of the dough cycle. If you have a Welbilt, DAK or Citizen machine with a hole in the pan, remove dough from pan and put it in a greased bowl. Seal bread machine pan or bowl with plastic wrap and refrigerate for about 30 minutes.

On a very lightly floured work surface, roll dough into a large rectangle. Spread softened butter evenly over dough, leaving a ½-inch border. Fold dough into thirds, as you would a business letter. Wrap dough in plastic wrap (or use a large plastic bag) and return to refrigerator for 30 minutes. Repeat this process 3 more times (4 foldings total; 2 hours total in the refrigerator).

After the final fold and the final 30-minute refrigeration, roll dough back into a large rectangle. With a sharp knife, pastry or pizza wheel, cut dough into squares of about 5 inches. Slice each square in half to form 2 triangles. Starting at the wide end, tightly roll dough so that the small, pointed end is on top and place on a lightly greased baking sheet. Cover and let rise in a warm, draft-free location for about 30 minutes. If baking the croissants in the morning, wrap baking sheet loosely in plastic and put it in the refrigerator. In the morning, remove croissants on baking sheet and let them come up to room temperature while you preheat the oven, about 20 minutes. Brush croissants with melted butter and bake in a preheated 350° oven for about 20 minutes or until golden.

per ¹⁄₁₂ **recipe**   *2399 calories, 13 g fat (8 g sat fat), 4 g protein, 26 g carbohydrate, 34 mg cholesterol, 105 mg sodium*

SCOTTISH ROWIES

These buttery breads are a cross between croissants and rolls and are truly decadent! Use butter and not margarine, as the margarine tends to leak out the sides too much during rolling.

DOUGH
1⅛ cups milk
2 tbs. butter
1 tbs. sugar
1 tsp. salt
3 cups all-purpose flour
1½ tsp. rapid or quick yeast

FILLING
½ cup butter, softened

Remove dough from the machine upon completion of the dough cycle and loosely wrap in a plastic bag or plastic wrap. Place in the refrigerator for 15 to 20 minutes — cold dough will be easier to handle.

Roll dough into a large rectangle on a lightly floured work surface. Spread butter evenly on top of dough and fold dough into thirds, as you would a business letter. Wrap folded dough in plastic wrap again and return to the refrigerator for 20 to 30 more minutes. Roll dough again into a large rectangle and fold into thirds. Wrap folded dough in plastic wrap and return to the refrigerator for 20 to 30 more minutes. Repeat this process one more time.

After the final refrigerated rise, roll dough into a large rectangle. With a knife, pastry or pizza wheel, cut dough into 2- to 3-inch squares. Place squares on a lightly greased baking sheet, cover and let rise for about 1 hour. Bake in a preheated 350° oven for 25 to 30 minutes or until puffed and golden.

per 1/12 **recipe**   *212 calories, 10 g fat (6 g sat fat), 4 g protein, 26 g carbohydrate, 26 mg cholesterol, 192 mg sodium*

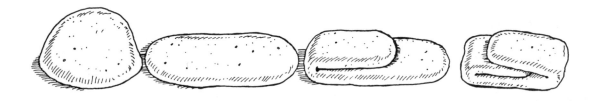

GERMAN FARM BREAD

Yield: 1 loaf or 12 rolls

This bread rises in a <u>banneton</u> or a muslin-lined basket, which leaves traditional ridges. Bannetons are available at large gourmet shops or through mail order catalogs. If you do not have one, use a medium-sized round woven basket or a large glass bowl. Place a 12- to 14-inch square piece of muslin in the basket or bowl and sprinkle it with 2 or 3 tbs. flour. Place the dough in the muslin-covered basket to rise and then turn onto a baking sheet or stone for baking. The dough will have indentations from the basket ridges.

DOUGH

1¼ cups water
2 tbs. butter or margarine
2 tbs. brown sugar
1 tsp. salt
½ cup whole wheat flour
½ cup rye flour
½ cup oats
2 cups bread flour
2 tsp. rapid or quick yeast

WASH
cold water

TOPPING
caraway seeds or other favorite seeds

For a loaf: Remove dough from the machine upon completion of the dough cycle. Place in a prepared *banneton* or basket to rise in a warm, draft-free location for about 2 hours or until double in bulk. Carefully turn loaf onto a greased baking sheet or stone so that the patterned side is up. Bake in a preheated 375° oven for about 30 minutes or until loaf is well browned and sounds hollow when tapped.

For rolls: Remove dough from the machine upon completion of the dough cycle and divide into 12 equal pieces. Shape each piece into a roll, place on a lightly greased baking sheet, cover and let rise for about 1 hour. Brush or spray rolls with cold water and sprinkle with caraway or other seeds if desired. Bake in a preheated 375° oven for about 20 minutes.

per ¹/₁₂ *recipe* *138 calories, 3 g fat (1 g sat fat), 4 g protein, 25 g carbohydrate, 0 mg cholesterol, 180 mg sodium*

MIDDLE EASTERN FLATBREAD (CHUREK)

Yield: 6 flatbreads

These Middle Eastern flatbreads are best eaten warm, right out of the oven. They do not rise for very long and are quick and easy to make. Eat warm with a meal or with cheese as a snack.

DOUGH
1⅛ cups water
2 tbs. olive oil
½ tsp. salt
3 cups bread flour
2 tsp. rapid or quick yeast

WASH
cold water

TOPPING
sesame seeds or other favorite seeds

Remove dough from the machine upon completion of the dough cycle and divide into 6 equal pieces. Roll each piece into a small, thin round and place on a lightly greased baking sheet. Cover and let rest for 10 to 15 minutes. Brush or spray with cold water and sprinkle with sesame seeds if desired. Bake in a preheated 350° oven for about 15 minutes.

per ⅙ recipe 242 calories, 6 g fat (1 g sat fat), 4 g protein, 40 g carbohydrate, 0 mg cholesterol, 179 mg sodium

CHALLAH

This Jewish egg bread is enjoyed by people of all religions any day of the year. If you want a really deep yellow color, use 2 yolks instead of 1 of the eggs, or just cheat a little and add some yellow food coloring.

DOUGH
¾ cup milk
2 tbs. butter or margarine
2 eggs
¼ cup sugar
1 tsp. salt
3 cups all-purpose flour
1½ tsp. rapid or quick yeast

WASH
1 egg mixed with 2 tbs. milk or cream

TOPPING
poppy seeds

Remove dough from the machine upon completion of the dough cycle. Divide dough into 3 equal pieces. On a lightly floured work surface, roll each piece into a long, slender rope. Braid the 3 ropes together (see page 10), place on a lightly greased baking sheet, cover and let rise in a warm, draft-free location for 1 to 1½ hours. Brush with egg wash, sprinkle with poppy seeds and bake in a preheated 350° oven until golden, about 25 to 30 minutes.

per ¹⁄₁₂ *recipe*   *166 calories, 3 g fat (2 g sat fat), 5 g protein, 29 g carbohydrate, 41 mg cholesterol, 197 mg sodium*

BUTTERFLAKE ROUNDS

These Middle Eastern breads remind me of a combination of croissants and pita breads! Eat warm with fruit preserves or cheese (or all by themselves!).

DOUGH
1 cup milk
2 tbs. butter
1 egg
1 tbs. sugar
½ tsp. salt
3 cups all-purpose flour
1½ tsp. rapid or quick yeast

FILLING
2 tbs. butter, melted

WASH
1 egg beaten with 2 tbs. milk or cream

TOPPING
sesame seeds

Remove dough from the machine upon completion of the dough cycle. Divide dough into 8 equal pieces and roll each into a large, thin round. Spread rounds with melted butter and roll each up tightly in jelly-roll fashion (see page 9). Coil each roll and flatten into a small round. Place flattened round on a greased baking sheet, cover and let rise for about 45 minutes. Wash with egg wash and sprinkle with sesame seeds. Bake in a preheated 350° oven for about 12 minutes or until golden.

per** ⅛ **recipe *249 calories, 7 g fat (4 g sat fat), 7 g protein, 39 g carbohydrate, 43 mg cholesterol, 159 mg sodium*

CHINESE STEAMED BUNS

Yield: about 24 buns

Steam these buns in a bamboo basket set in a covered wok (in traditional Chinese fashion), or in a vegetable steamer, and serve hot with meat.

1⅛ cups water
1 tbs. brown sugar
3 cups all-purpose flour
1½ tsp. rapid or quick yeast

Remove dough from the machine upon completion of the dough cycle. Form dough into about 24 equal balls, place on a lightly greased baking sheet or waxed paper, cover and let rest for about 20 minutes. Meanwhile, bring water to a boil in the bottom of the steamer. Place rolls in steamer basket, leaving at least 1 inch between rolls. Steam rolls for about 10 minutes or until firm and cooked through. The rolls may be resteamed if necessary. Serve hot.

per ¹⁄₂₄ *recipe*   *60 calories, 0 g fat (0 g sat fat), 2 g protein, 13 g carbohydrate, 0 mg cholesterol, 1 mg sodium*

HOLIDAY BREADS

ITALIAN SWEET WREATH 139
MIDDLE EASTERN FILLED HOLIDAY BUNS . . 140
GREEK HOLIDAY BREAD 142
HOT CROSS BUNS 143
EASTER BAGELS (TADALE) 144
GREEK EASTER BREAD (TSOUREKI) 145
TURKISH EASTER BREAD 146
DANISH CHRISTMAS BREAD (JULKAGE) . . . 147
GERMAN STOLLEN 148
SCANDINAVIAN SWEET BREAD (PULLA) . . . 150
ST. LUCIA BUNS 151
BREAD OF THE KINGS 152
GREEK NEW YEAR BREAD (VASILOPITA) . . . 154

ITALIAN SWEET WREATH

Yield: 1 loaf

This recipe is based on a recipe for an Italian Corona Dolce, or a sweet wreath, which is served at holiday times. The flavorful topping makes this bread stand apart.

DOUGH
1⅓ cups water
2 tbs. butter or margarine
2 tbs. sugar
1 tsp. salt
4 cups all-purpose flour
2 tsp. rapid or quick yeast

TOPPING
¼ cup sugar
1 tsp. cinnamon
1 tsp. anise seed
⅛ tsp. nutmeg

WASH
1 egg beaten with 2 tbs. water

Remove dough from the machine upon completion of the dough cycle and place on a lightly floured work surface. Divide dough into 3 equal pieces, roll each piece into a long, slender rope and braid ropes together (see page 10). Shape braid into a wreath-shaped circle and pinch ends together to seal. Place on a lightly greased baking sheet. Cover and let rise for 30 to 40 minutes in a warm, draft-free location. Mix topping ingredients together. Brush top with egg wash and sprinkle with topping. Bake in a preheated 350° oven for about 20 minutes or until golden brown.

per ¹⁄₁₂ **recipe**   195 calories, 2 g fat 10 g sat fat), 5 g protein, 38 g carbohydrate, 5 mg cholesterol, 180 mg sodium

MIDDLE EASTERN FILLED HOLIDAY BUNS

*These sweet rolls are traditional for both Easter and Christmas. Mahlab is part of the seed of the black cherry and must be crushed with a mortar and pestle. It is possible that you can find it at a Middle Eastern restaurant, but the easiest way to find it is by mail order (see **Sources**, page 165). Allspice may be used as a substitute. Start with 3 cups flour and add more if necessary to obtain the right consistency.*

DOUGH
1/2 cup water
1/4 cup vegetable oil
3 eggs
2 tbs. sugar
1 tsp. salt
1-2 tsp. ground mahlab or allspice
3-3 1/4 cups all-purpose flour
2 tsp. rapid or quick yeast

FILLING
1/2 cup finely chopped dates
1/2 cup finely ground almonds
1 tsp. cinnamon
1/2 tsp. nutmeg
about 2 tbs. honey

WASH
1 egg beaten with 1 tbs. milk

While dough is rising in the machine, make filling. In a medium bowl, combine dates, almonds, cinnamon and nutmeg. Add honey. With your hands, mix until filling is well blended; set aside.

Upon completion of the dough cycle, remove dough from machine. If dough is sticky, knead in only enough flour so that it is easily handled. Divide into 12 to 15 equal pieces. Form each piece into a ball and stuff each one with a large spoonful of filling (see page 11). Pinch ends together to seal. Place rolls in greased muffin cups. Cover and let rise in a warm, draft-free location for about 30 minutes. Brush with egg wash. Bake in a preheated 350° oven for 15 to 20 minutes.

per 1/12 *recipe* 246 calories, 9 g fat (1 g sat fat), 6 g protein, 36 g carbohydrate, 53 mg cholesterol, 196 mg sodium

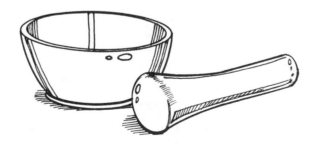

GREEK HOLIDAY BREAD

Yield: 1 loaf

*This holiday bread is either braided or made into a simple round loaf and stamped with a floured church seal before rising. Mahlab is part of the seed of the black cherry and must be crushed with a mortar and pestle (see **Sources**, page 165).*

DOUGH
⅔ cup milk
2 tbs. butter or margarine
2 eggs
½ cup sugar
1 tsp. salt
½ tsp. cinnamon
1 tsp. ground mahlab or allspice
3 cups all-purpose flour
2 tsp. rapid or quick yeast

WASH
1 egg yolk beaten with 1-2 tbs. milk

TOPPING
almond meal (finely ground almonds)

Remove dough from the machine upon completion of the dough cycle and divide into 3 equal pieces. Roll each piece on a lightly floured work surface into a long, slender rope. Braid ropes together (see page 10), place on a lightly greased baking sheet, cover and let rise in a warm, draft-free location for about 1 hour. Brush with egg wash and sprinkle liberally with almond meal. Bake in a preheated 350° oven until golden, about 25 to 30 minutes.

per ¹⁄₁₂ *recipe*   182 calories, 3 g fat (2 g sat fat), 5 g protein, 33 g carbohydrate, 41 mg cholesterol, 197 mg sodium

HOT CROSS BUNS

Yield: 12 buns

Traditionally eaten all over the world on Good Friday, these buns have a cross made with a powdered sugar glaze on top. This variation uses dried fruits.

DOUGH

⅞ cup (7 oz.) milk
2 tbs. butter or margarine
1 egg
¼ cup sugar
1 tsp. salt

1 tsp. lemon or orange peel or
 1 tsp. cinnamon
3 cups all-purpose flour
1½ tsp. rapid or quick yeast
ADD: ½ cup dried fruits of choice

GLAZE

Powdered Sugar Glaze with vanilla, almond or orange extract, page 158

Add fruit to the machine pan after dough ball has been formed, about 5 to 8 minutes into the kneading phase. Remove dough from machine upon completion of the dough cycle. Divide dough into 12 equal pieces, shape into small balls and place in lightly greased muffin cups. Cover and let rise for about 1 hour in a warm, draft-free location. Just before baking, score a cross into the top of each bun with a sharp razor blade or knife. Bake in a preheated 350° oven for 15 to 20 minutes. While buns are still warm, drizzle glaze into cross on top of each bun.

per ¹⁄₁₂ recipe   187 calories, 3 g fat (1 g sat fat), 5 g protein, 35 g carbohydrate, 23 mg cholesterol, 194 mg sodium

EASTER BAGELS (TADALE)

Yield: 12 bagels

Donna Harrington always made her grandmother's recipe by hand for Easter to give to friends. She can now make it by machine. The original recipe calls for shortening instead of butter. These are really rich and delicious!

¾ cup milk
5 tbs. butter or shortening
1 egg
½ cup sugar

½ tsp. salt
1½ tsp. anise seed, or to taste
3½ cups all-purpose flour
2 tsp. rapid or quick yeast

Remove dough from the machine upon completion of the dough cycle and divide into 12 equal balls. Shape dough like bagels by forming a bun, pushing a hole in the middle with your thumb and stretching it a little (see page 87). Drop bagels into gently boiling water a few at a time. When they come to the top, they are ready to bake. Place on the bottom rack of the oven or directly on a pizza stone. Bake in a preheated 350° oven for 30 to 35 minutes or until golden brown.

per 1/12 **recipe** *221 calories, 6 g fat (3 g sat fat), 5 g protein, 37 g carbohydrate, 31 mg cholesterol, 104 mg sodium*

GREEK EASTER BREAD (TSOUREKI)

Yield: 1 braided loaf

This version of tsoureki is made with crushed anise seeds (use a mortar and a pestle) although mahlab is also frequently used. Yellow food coloring may be added to the milk, or use two egg yolks instead of the whole egg for a deeper, yellow color.

DOUGH

¾ cup milk
¼ cup butter or margarine
1 egg
¼ cup sugar
1 tsp. salt

1 tsp. dried lemon peel, or freshly grated to taste
1 tsp. ground anise seeds
3 cups all-purpose flour
2 tsp. rapid or quick yeast

WASH

1 egg yolk beaten with 1-2 tbs. milk

Remove dough from the machine upon completion of the dough cycle. Divide dough into 3 equal pieces and roll each piece on a lightly floured work surface into a long, slender rope. Braid ropes together, place on a lightly greased baking sheet, cover and let rise in a warm, draft-free location for about 1 hour. Brush with egg yolk wash and bake in a preheated 350° oven until golden, about 25 to 30 minutes.

per ¹⁄₁₂ recipe   178 calories, 5 g fat (3 g sat fat), 5 g protein, 29 g carbohydrate, 28 mg cholesterol, 192 mg sodium

TURKISH EASTER BREAD

The mahlab (see page 140) may be replaced with allspice. Add yellow food coloring to the milk for a deeper color if desired.

DOUGH
1 cup milk
2 tbs. butter or margarine
1 egg yolk
1/4 cup sugar
1 tsp. salt
1 tsp. ground mahlab or allspice
3 cups all-purpose flour
2 tsp. rapid or quick yeast

WASH
1 egg yolk beaten with 1-2 tbs. milk or cream

TOPPING
finely chopped almonds or hazelnuts

Upon completion of the dough cycle, remove dough from the machine. Divide dough into 3 equal pieces and roll each piece on a lightly floured work surface into a long, slender rope. Braid ropes together (see page 10), place on a lightly greased baking sheet, cover and let rise in a warm, draft-free location for 1 to 1 1/2 hours. Brush with egg yolk wash, sprinkle with nuts and bake in a preheated 350° oven until golden, about 25 to 30 minutes.

per 1/12 recipe   161 calories, 3 g fat (1 g sat fat), 4 g protein, 30 g carbohydrate, 23 mg cholesterol, 190 mg sodium

DANISH CHRISTMAS BREAD (JULKAGE)

Yield: 1 loaf

*This Danish Christmas bread is similar to **Pulla** but contains dried fruits and nuts.*

DOUGH

1 cup milk
1 egg
2 tbs. butter or margarine
1 tsp. vanilla extract
1/4 cup sugar
1 tsp. salt
1/2 tsp. cinnamon

1/2 tsp. dried lemon peel, or freshly
   grated to taste
1/2 tsp. ground cardamom
3 cups all-purpose flour
2 tsp. rapid or quick yeast
ADD: 1/2 cup dried fruits (raisins, cherries)
ADD: 1/4-1/2 cup chopped almonds

WASH

1 egg beaten with 2 tbs. milk or cream

Add dried fruits and nuts to the machine pan about 5 minutes after kneading has started. Remove dough from the machine upon completion of the dough cycle and divide into 3 equal pieces. Roll each piece into a long rope and braid ropes together (see page 10). Place braid on a lightly greased baking pan, cover and let rise for about 1 1/2 hours. Brush dough with egg wash and bake in a preheated 350° oven for 25 to 30 minutes or until golden.

per 1/12 recipe *199 calories, 4 g fat (2 g sat fat), 5 g protein, 35 g carbohydrate, 23 mg cholesterol, 196 mg sodium*

GERMAN STOLLEN

Yield: 1 loaf

A traditional Christmas bread, stollen is often packed with candied orange peels, citron or dried fruits. This adaptation uses dried fruits. Because of the high amount of sugar, this bread is a heavy, dense loaf that does not rise very high, even with a long rising time.

DOUGH

¼ cup orange juice
¾ cup milk
2 tbs. butter or margarine
1 tsp. rum extract
1 tsp. almond extract
¼ cup sugar
½ tsp. salt
1 tsp. dried orange peel, or freshly grated to taste
½ tsp. cinnamon
3 cups all-purpose flour
2 tsp. rapid or quick yeast
ADD: ¼ cup golden raisins
ADD: ¼-⅓ cup dried cherries, blueberries, dried cranberries or a combination
ADD: ¼-⅓ cup chopped almonds

GLAZE
Orange Glaze or *Powdered Sugar Glaze*, page 158

Add fruits and nuts to the machine pan after dough has formed a ball, about 5 minutes into the first kneading. Allow dough to sit in the machine undisturbed for about 2 hours after completion of the dough cycle. If you have a 1 lb. machine, place dough in a large, greased bowl, cover it and place it in a warm draft-free location. Because dough is so heavy, it will not rise very high. Remove dough from machine upon completion of the dough cycle and roll it into a thick 8-x-12-inch oval on a lightly floured work surface. Fold dough in half lengthwise with the top half folding over about ¾ of the bottom, and press to seal seams together. Place on a lightly greased baking sheet, cover and let rise in a warm, draft-free location for about 2 hours. Bake in a preheated 350° oven until golden, about 35 to 40 minutes.

per 1/12 *recipe*   194 calories, 4 g fat (1 g sat fat), 5 g protein, 36 g carbohydrate, 5 mg cholesterol, 100 mg sodium

SCANDINAVIAN SWEET BREAD (PULLA)

Yield: 1 loaf

This Scandinavian sweet bread is often served at Christmas time and is either braided or made into animal shapes. Ground cardamom seeds are common in Northern European sweets and breads.

DOUGH

1 cup milk
2 tbs. butter or margarine
1 egg
1 tsp. vanilla or almond extract
1/4 cup sugar

1 tsp. salt
1/2-1 tsp. ground cardamom
3 cups all-purpose flour
2 tsp. rapid or quick yeast

WASH

1 egg beaten with 2 tbs. milk or cream

Remove dough from the machine upon completion of the dough cycle and divide into 3 equal pieces. Roll each piece into a long rope and braid ropes together (see page 10). Place braid on a lightly greased baking pan, cover and let rise for about 1½ hours. Brush dough with egg wash and bake in a preheated 350° oven for 25 to 30 minutes or until golden.

per 1/12 *recipe* *162 calories, 3 g fat (1 g sat fat), 5 g protein, 29 g carbohydrate, 23 mg cholesterol, 195 mg sodium*

ST. LUCIA BUNS

These buns are traditionally served to Swedish families by the eldest daughter at dawn on December 13th. However, they may be enjoyed any day of the year.

DOUGH
pinch saffron, or 1-2 drops yellow
  food coloring
1 cup milk
1/4 cup butter
1 tsp. vanilla extract
1/3 cup sugar
1/2 tsp. salt
3 cups all-purpose flour
2 tsp. rapid or quick yeast

WASH
1 egg beaten with 1-2 tbs. cream or milk

TOPPING
a few raisins

Remove dough from the machine upon completion of the dough cycle. Divide into 24 equal pieces and roll into long, slender ropes. Using 2 ropes for each bun, make an X and then coil dough (see page 6). Place on a greased baking sheet, cover and let rise for about 40 to 50 minutes. Brush with egg wash and place a few raisins decoratively in center of coils. Bake in a preheated 350° oven until golden, about 20 to 25 minutes.

per 1/12 recipe   *178 calories, 4 g fat (2 g sat fat), 4 g protein, 31 g carbohydrate, 11mg cholesterol, 101 mg sodium*

BREAD OF THE KINGS

This bread is traditionally eaten in both Spain and Mexico on Epiphany (January 6). There is a cake-like version that is also eaten in New Orleans but it is not a yeast-raised product. Hidden in the bread (or cake) is a small trinket or coin (I use a nut), which brings good luck to the person who finds it. I use either fruit bits (from the grocery store) or a combination of dried cherries, blueberries and golden raisins.

DOUGH
1 cup milk
1 egg
3 tbs. butter or margarine
1 tsp. vanilla or almond extract
1 tsp. salt
¼ cup sugar
1 tsp. dried lemon peel, or freshly grated to taste
3½ cups all-purpose flour
2 tsp. rapid or quick yeast
ADD: ½ cup mixed dried fruits

ADDITIONAL INGREDIENT
1 small nut (½ almond or pecan or ¼ walnut)

WASH
1 egg beaten with 1-2 tbs. milk

Add fruits to the machine pan after the dough ball has formed, about 5 to 8 minutes after the kneading starts. Heavily grease a Bundt or angel food cake pan. Upon completion of the dough cycle, remove dough from machine and push nut into dough. Shape and place dough in prepared pan. Cover with a kitchen towel and let rise for 1½ to 2 hours in a warm, draft-free location. Bake in a preheated 350° oven for about 30 minutes or until nicely browned. Cool on a wire rack.

per ¹⁄₁₂ *recipe*   201 calories, 4 g fat (2 g sat fat), 5 g protein, 36 g carbohydrate, 26 mg cholesterol, 196 mg sodium

GREEK NEW YEAR BREAD (VASILOPITA)

Yield: 1 loaf

*Like **Bread of the Kings**, a coin (in years past a gold one) is hidden inside this loaf of bread, which is eaten at midnight on New Year's Eve. The one who finds the coin, according to tradition, is blessed with luck during the New Year.*

DOUGH

⅞ cup (7 oz.) milk
1 egg
2 tbs. butter or margarine
2 tsp. almond extract
½ cup sugar
1 tsp. salt
1 tsp. ground mahlab or allspice
1 tsp. cinnamon
1 tsp. dried orange peel, or freshly grated to taste
3 cups all-purpose flour
2 tsp. rapid or quick yeast

ADDITIONAL INGREDIENT
1 small nut (½ almond or pecan or ¼ walnut)

WASH
1 egg yolk beaten with 1-2 tbs. milk or cream

TOPPING
sliced or chopped almonds

Remove dough from the machine upon completion of the dough cycle. Roll dough into a large rectangle on a floured work surface. Add only enough flour to prevent sticking. Place a small nut somewhere on the dough. With scissors, a sharp knife or a pastry or pizza wheel, cut 1-inch strips down both sides of the dough from the center third to the side. Fold down a 1-inch piece of dough over the center third and then alternately fold side strips over, angling each folded strip down. Tuck ends inside to give the appearance of a braid (see *Mock braid*, page 10). Place on a greased baking sheet, cover and let rise in a warm, draft-free location for about 1 hour. Brush with egg yolk wash, sprinkle with nuts and bake in a preheated 350° oven until golden, about 30 to 35 minutes.

per $\frac{1}{12}$ ***recipe*** *179 calories, 3 g fat (1 g sat fat), 5 g protein, 34 g carbohydrate, 23 mg cholesterol, 194 mg sodium*

FINISHING TOUCHES

ABOUT GLAZES AND BUTTERS 157
POWDERED SUGAR GLAZE 158
ORANGE GLAZE 158
COCONUT GLAZE 159
RUM GLAZE 159
FRUIT GLAZE 160
LEMON GLAZE 160
WALNUT BUTTER 161
ORANGE GINGER BUTTER 161
BASIL BUTTER 162
CRANBUTTER 162
SPICY HONEY BUTTER 163
ORANGE CHEESE SPREAD 163
HERBED YOGURT CHEESE SPREAD 164

ABOUT GLAZES AND BUTTERS

A *glaze* is spread over the cooked bread while it is still warm. While glazes may be applied with a pastry brush, it is very common to simply pour the glaze over an entire loaf of bread or to spoon the glaze on top of rolls or shaped breads. Glazes are typically sweet and used on rich and/or sweet breads.

Butters and *spreads* are very easy to make and can be that special finishing touch for bread. For gifts or for special meals, chill the butters in fancy little shapes or fill small ramekins or decorative jars. Flavored butters can be wrapped tightly in plastic or wrapped paper and frozen for 6 weeks or refrigerated for about 1 week.

Butter logs or rolls are easily made by placing the butter on a piece of plastic wrap and rolling it up into a roll. Twist the ends and tie closed. Chill until firm, about 1 hour.

Butters molded with cookie cutters are extremely easy to make for a great presentation. Select a (holiday-shaped) cookie cutter that is open on both top and bottom. Spray it with nonstick vegetable spray and place on a piece of waxed paper. Fill with butter and refrigerate for several hours. When firm, carefully push the butter out of the cutter onto a small plate to serve.

Butter molds can be found in gourmet shops or mail order catalogs. Follow the directions that come with the molds.

POWDERED SUGAR GLAZE

This is the basis for literally hundreds of variations of glazes. While the common extract used is vanilla, try almond, lemon, coconut or rum to complement the flavor of the bread. The thicker the glaze, the heavier it will be. A light glaze will pour easily.

½ cup confectioners' sugar
1-2 tbs. milk
½ tsp. extract

Mix ingredients together in a small bowl. Adjust consistency with milk as desired.

ORANGE GLAZE

Orange juice may be substituted for the concentrate, but it will have less orange flavor.

½ cup confectioners' sugar
1-2 tbs. frozen orange juice concentrate

1 tsp. orange extract
½ tsp. orange peel

Mix ingredients together in a small bowl. Adjust consistency with juice concentrate as desired.

COCONUT GLAZE

Try this glaze with any chocolate or coconut breads.

½ cup confectioners' sugar
¼ cup coconut flakes

2-3 tbs. milk
1 tsp. coconut extract

Mix ingredients together in a small bowl. Adjust consistency with milk as desired.

RUM GLAZE

If you prefer, you may use ½ tbs. rum extract and a little water as a substitute for the rum.

½ cup confectioners' sugar
1 tbs. rum
1 tbs. melted butter

Mix ingredients together in a small bowl. Adjust consistency with rum or water as desired.

FRUIT GLAZE

This simple glaze gives breads a festive, holiday presentation — great for gifts.

½ cup fruit preserves or jam (apricot, orange, etc.)
1 tbs. brandy

Melt preserves or jam in the top of a double boiler over low heat. Remove from heat, stir in brandy and strain through cheesecloth into a small bowl. Apply strained glaze while bread is still warm.

LEMON GLAZE

Use this as a special finishing touch for any bread which contains lemon peel.

½ cup confectioners' sugar
1-2 tbs. lemon juice
1 tsp. almond extract
dried lemon peel, or freshly grated to taste

Mix ingredients together in a small bowl. Adjust consistency with lemon juice as desired.

WALNUT BUTTER

*This is really delicious spread on top of **Walnut Raisin Cinnamon Rolls**, page 61. I use walnuts, but any other nut may be used as a variation. The light toasting enhances the flavor of the nuts.*

½ cup walnut pieces   1 tbs. honey
½ cup unsalted butter, softened

Spread nuts on a greased baking sheet and bake in a preheated 350° oven for about 10 minutes. Cool. Process cooled nuts with a food processor until finely chopped. Add softened butter and honey; process until blended.

ORANGE GINGER BUTTER

This may be eaten on just about any bread, and could also be served with vegetables.

½ cup butter, softened   ½-1 tsp. chopped ginger
¼ cup orange marmalade

Cream butter in a mixer or food processor. Add remaining ingredients and process until well blended. Chill for at least 1 hour to set. Serve chilled or at room temperature.

BASIL BUTTER

This is a great accompaniment to any herb roll or bread. Any fresh herb (such as mint, parsley or cilantro) can be used instead of the basil.

½ cup butter, softened
¼ cup lightly packed basil leaves

½ tsp. coarsely ground pepper

Cream butter in a mixer or food processor. Add remaining ingredients and process until well blended. Chill for at least 1 hour to set. Serve chilled or at room temperature.

CRANBUTTER

This is a sweet butter spread for a fall breakfast treat or with sweet rolls for Thanksgiving dinner.

½ cup butter, softened
¼ cup confectioners' sugar
3-4 mandarin orange segments

½ tsp. orange peel
¼ cup fresh cranberries

Cream butter in a mixer or food processor. Add remaining ingredients and process until well blended. Chill for at least 1 hour to set. Serve chilled or at room temperature.

SPICY HONEY BUTTER

Apple pie or pumpkin pie spice adds pizzazz to ordinary honey butter.

1/2 cup butter, softened
2 tbs. honey
1 tsp. apple or pumpkin pie spice

Cream butter in a mixer or food processor. Add remaining ingredients and process until well blended. Chill for at least 1 hour to set. Serve chilled or at room temperature.

ORANGE CHEESE SPREAD

This dresses up any sweet roll.

4 oz. cream cheese, softened
1/2 cup confectioners' sugar
1 tsp. orange peel

1-2 tbs. frozen orange juice
   concentrate, thawed

Put cream cheese in a mixer or food processor. Add remaining ingredients and mix or process until well blended. Chill for at least 1 hour to set. Serve chilled or at room temperature.

HERBED YOGURT CHEESE SPREAD

Yogurt cheese rather than butter is used as a base for this healthful and delicious spread. You can also add flavored extracts and fruits to yogurt cheese for sweet spreads and dessert toppings. There are yogurt cheese makers available through many kitchen or gourmet shops, but a simple colander can also be used. The whey can be used in bread making as a dough enhancer and conditioner. Add 1-2 tsp. to the bottom of the measuring cup before adding the liquid.

½ cup yogurt cheese*
1 tsp. or 1 clove minced garlic
½ tsp. coarse black pepper
¼ cup chopped fresh herbs

Stir finely chopped herbs into yogurt cheese and chill.

*To make yogurt cheese: Line a small colander with several thicknesses of coffee filters and rest the colander over a small bowl. Place nonfat yogurt *without gelatin* in the colander and refrigerate for several hours. The whey will drain into the bowl, leaving a thick yogurt with a consistency similar to softened cream cheese. Yield is about half, or 1 cup yogurt cheese from 2 cups yogurt.

SOURCES

Call for a catalog or price list.

FLOURS AND GRAINS

Arrowhead Mills, TX	806-364-0730	Gray's Grist Mill, RI	508-636-6075
Birket Mills, NY	315-536-3311	Great River Organic Milling, MN	507-457-0334
Bob's Red Mill		Kenyon's Corn Meal Co., RI	401-783-4054
Natural Foods, OR	503-654-3215	King Arthur's Flour, VT	800-827-6836
Brewster River Mill, VT	802-644-2987	Old Mill of Guilford, NC	919-643-4783
Brumwell Milling, IA	319-578-8106	Pamela's Products, CA	415-952-4546
Country Harvest, UT	800-322-2245	Paul's Grains, IA	515-476-3373
Garden Spot Dist., PA	800-829-5100	Tadco/Niblack, NY	800-724-8883

SPICES AND DRIED FRUITS

American Spoons, MI	800-222-5886	Penzey's Spice House, WI	414-574-0277
Chukar Cherries, WA	800-624-9544	The Spice House, WI	414-272-0977
House of Spices, NY	718-476-1577	Tadco/Niblack, NY	800-724-8883
King Arthur Baking Catalog, VT	800-827-6836		

BIBLIOGRAPHY

Algar, Ayla. CLASSICAL TURKISH COOKING. New York: HarperCollins, 1991.

Anderson, Jean and Wurz, Hedy. THE NEW GERMAN COOKBOOK. New York: HarperCollins, 1993.

Bayless, Rick and Bayless, Deann Groen. AUTHENTIC MEXICAN. New York: William Morrow, 1987.

Beard, James. BEARD ON BREAD. New York: Ballantine Books, 1981.

Casas, Penelope. THE FOODS AND WINES OF SPAIN. New York: Alfred A. Knopf, 1988.

Chririnian, Linda. SECRETS OF COOKING ARMENIAN/LEBANESE/PERSIAN. (TOWN?),CT: Leonhart, 1987.

Clayton, Bernard. NEW COMPLETE BOOK OF BREADS. New York: Simon and Schuster, 1987.

Duff, Gail. BREAD 150 TRADITIONAL RECIPES FROM AROUND THE WORLD. New York: Macmillan, 1993.

Gisslen, Wayne. PROFESSIONAL BAKING. New York: John Wiley and Sons, 1985.

Hong, Mariana. BREADS OF THE WORLD. New York: Chelsea House, 1977.

Jones, Judith and Evan. THE BOOK OF BREAD. New York: Harper and Row, 1982.

Mallos, Tess. THE COMPLETE MIDDLE EAST COOKBOOK. Rutland, VT: Charles E. Tuttle, 1993.

Oppenneer, Betsy. THE BREAD BOOK. New York: HarperCollins, 1994.

Ortiz, Elizabeth Labert. THE COMPLETE BOOK OF MEXICAN COOKING. New York: M. Evans, 1967.

Pappas, Lou Seibert. BREAD BAKING. San Leandro, CA: Bristol Publishing Enterprises, 1975.

Roden, Claudia. A BOOK OF MIDDLE EASTERN FOOD. New York: Vintage Books, 1968.

Sands, Brinna. THE KING ARTHUR FLOUR 200TH ANNIVERSARY COOKBOOK. Woodstock, VT: Countryman Press, 1992.

Salloum, Mary. A TASTE OF LEBANON. New York: Interlink Books, 1988.

von Bremzen, Anya and Welchman, John. PLEASE TO THE TABLE. New York: Workman, 1990.

INDEX

Almond apricot English muffins
94
Anise sesame rolls 121
Apple cinnamon raisin bagels 91
Armenian rolls 118

Bagels
  apple cinnamon raisin 91
  cinnamon raisin 91
  directions 87
  Easter (tadale) 144
  egg 88
  onion 90
  orange raisin 90
  plain 88
  pumpernickel 89
  whole wheat 89
Baguettes
  jalapeño cheese cornmeal 38
  Mexican-flavored 36
  orange ginger 40
  Parmesan pepper 44

simple 33
sponge 34
tomato herb 42
Basil butter 162
Beer breadsticks 48
Beignets 100
Bibliography 166
Bread of the kings 152
Breadsticks
  beer 48
  Italian (grissini) 46
  jalapeño cheese cornmeal 38
  Mexican-flavored 36
  orange ginger 40
  Parmesan pepper 44
  tomato herb 42
Brioche 20
Butterflake rounds 136
Butters
  basil 162
  cranbutter 162
  orange ginger 161

spicy honey 163
walnut 161

Caramel almond buns 58
Challah 135
Cheese
  brioche 20
  -filled herb rolls 28
  herb-filled loaf 24
  herbed monkey bread 32
  herbed yogurt cheese
    spread 164
  jalapeño cornmeal baguettes
    or breadsticks 38
  lemon crescents 72
  potato rye rolls 26
  scallion bread 23
  yogurt 25, 164
Chinese steamed buns 137
Chocolate doughnuts 101
Cinnamon
  buns 54

Cinnamon, continued
    raisin bagels 91
    raisin English muffins 94
Citizen bread machine 3
Coconut
    chocolate rolls 66
    doughnuts 102
    glaze 159
Coffee cake
    German 81
    Moravian 80
    sour cream 84
    streusel-topped 82
Cornmeal
    jalapeño baguettes or
      breadsticks 38
Cranbutter 162
Croissants 128
Crumpets 96
Crust treatments 13-15

DAK bread machine 3
Danish Christmas bread
    (julkage)147

Double chocolate rolls 65
Dough
    crust treatments 13-15
    embellishments 13
    freezing 4
    refrigerating 4
    shaping 5-12
    washes 13
Dough cycle directions 2
Doughnuts
    basic 98
    chocolate 101
    coconut 102

Easter bagels 144
Egg bagels 88
Embellishments 13
English muffins
    almond apricot 94
    basic 92
    cinnamon raisin 94
    directions 92
    Hawaiian-style 95
    orange raisin 93

whole wheat 93

Fastnachts 104
Flatbread
    French (fougasse) 110
    Indian (naan) 113
    Mediterranean cheese 122
    Middle Eastern (churek) 134
    Persian 112
    pita 111
French
    flatbread (fougasse) 110
    walnut rolls 124
Fried Mexican sweet rolls
    (sopaipillas) 97
Fruit glaze 160

German
    coffee cake 81
    coffee crescents 76
    farm bread 132
    sour cream sweet rolls 78
    stollen 148

Glazes
    about 157
    coconut 159
    fruit 160
    lemon 160
    orange 158
    powdered sugar 158
    rum 159
Golden Valencian rolls 125
Greek
    Easter bread (tsoureki) 145
    holiday bread 142
    New Year bread (vasilopita) 154
    psomi 108

Hawaiian
    nut crescents 70
    pineapple rolls 22
    -style English muffins 95
Herb(ed)
    -filled loaf 24
    rolls 30
    monkey bread 32

yogurt cheese spread 164
Holiday breads
    bread of the kings 152
    Danish Christmas (julkage) 147
    Easter bagels 144
    German stollen 148
    Greek 142
    Greek Easter (tsoureki) 145
    Greek New Year (vasilopita) 154
    hot cross buns 143
    Italian sweet wreath 139
    Middle Eastern filled buns 140
    Scandinavian sweet (pulla) 150
    Turkish Easter 146
Honey
    buns 64
    butter, spicy 163
Hot cross buns 143

Indian flatbread (naan) 113
Italian
    breadsticks (grissini) 46
    sweet wreath 139

Jalapeño cheese cornmeal
    baguettes or breadsticks 38

Kaiser rolls 114
Kugelhopf 127

Lemon
    crescents 72
    glaze 160
Loaf
    bread of the kings 152
    challah 135
    cheese scallion bread 23
    Danish Christmas bread (julkage) 147
    German farm bread 132
    German stollen 148
    Greek Easter bread (tsoureki) 145
    Greek holiday bread 142
    Greek New Year bread 154
    herb-filled 24
    herbed monkey bread 32
    Italian sweet wreath 139

Loaf, continued
    kugelhopf 127
    olive walnut bread 31
    Scandinavian sweet bread
        (pulla) 150
    Swedish chocolate bread 67
    sweet monkey bread 53
    Turkish Easter bread 146

Mahlab rings 119
Masa harina
    Mexican-flavored baguettes
        or breadsticks 36
Mediterranean cheese flat-
        bread 122
Mexican
    chocolate rolls 68
    -flavored baguettes or
        breadsticks 36
    rolls, crusty (bolillos and
        teleras) 106
    sweet rolls (pan dulce) 116
Middle Eastern
    filled holiday buns 140

flatbread (churek) 134
    sesame rings (simit) 115
Monkey bread
    herbed 32
    sweet 53
Moravian coffee cake 80

Oats
    apple cinnamon raisin
        bagels 91
    German farm bread 132
    pumpkin rolls 69
Olive walnut bread 31
Onion bagels 90
Orange
    cheese spread 163
    craisin buns 56
    ginger baguettes or bread-
        sticks 40
    ginger butter 161
    glaze 158
    raisin bagels 90
    raisin English muffins 93

Parker House rolls 19
Parmesan pepper baguettes or
        breadsticks 44
Persian flatbread 112
Pita bread 111
Plain bagels 88
Poppy seed-filled rolls 74
Potato
    cinnamon rolls 60
    rye cheese rolls 26
Powdered sugar glaze 158
Pretzels 49
Pumpernickel bagels 89
Pumpkin rolls 69

Rolls
    brioche 20
    cheese-filled herb 28
    Chinese steamed buns 137
    croissants 128
    crusty Mexican (bolillos and
        teleras) 106
    French walnut 124
    Hawaiian pineapple 22

Rolls, continued
   herb 30
   Kaiser 114
   Parker House 19
   potato rye cheese 26
   Scottish rowies 130
Rosemary raisin bread 120
Rum glaze 159
Rye
   German farm bread 132
   potato cheese rolls 26
   pumpernickel bagels 89

Scandinavian sweet bread
   (pulla) 150
Scottish rowies 130
Simple baguettes 33
Sour cream coffee cake 84
Sources 165
Spanish sugar rolls 126
Sponge baguettes 34
Spreads
   herbed yogurt cheese 164
   orange cheese 163

St. Lucia buns 151
Sticky buns 62
Streusel-topped coffee cake 80
Swedish chocolate bread 65
Sweet rolls 52
   anise sesame 121
   Armenian 118
   caramel almond buns 58
   cinnamon buns 54
   coconut chocolate 66
   double chocolate 65
   German coffee crescents 76
   German sour cream 78
   golden Valencian 125
   Hawaiian nut crescents 70
   honey buns 64
   hot cross buns 143
   lemon crescents 72
   Mexican (pan dulce) 116
   Mexican chocolate 68
   orange craisin buns 56
   poppy seed-filled 74
   potato cinnamon 60
   pumpkin 69

Spanish sugar 126
St. Lucia buns 151
sticky buns 62
walnut raisin cinnamon 61

Tomato herb baguettes or
   breadsticks 42
Turkish Easter bread 146

Walnut
   butter 161
   raisin cinnamon rolls 61
Washes 13
Welbilt 100 bread machine 3
West Indian floats 103
Whole wheat
   bagels 89
   English muffins 93
   German farm bread 132
   potato rye cheese rolls 26
   pumpernickel bagels 89

Yogurt cheese 25, 164

Serve creative, easy, nutritious meals with nitty gritty® cookbooks

Wraps and Roll-Ups
Easy Vegetarian Cooking
Party Fare: Irresistible Nibbles
  for Every Occasion
Cappuccino/Espresso: The Book of
  Beverages
Fresh Vegetables
Cooking with Fresh Herbs
Cooking with Chile Peppers
The Dehydrator Cookbook
Recipes for the Pressure Cooker
Beer and Good Food
Unbeatable Chicken Recipes
Gourmet Gifts
From Freezer, 'Fridge and Pantry
Edible Pockets for Every Meal
Oven and Rotisserie Roasting
Risottos, Paellas and Other Rice
  Specialties
Muffins, Nut Breads and More
Healthy Snacks for Kids
100 Dynamite Desserts
Recipes for Yogurt Cheese
Sautés
Cooking in Porcelain

Casseroles
The Toaster Oven Cookbook
Skewer Cooking on the Grill
Creative Mexican Cooking
Marinades
No Salt, No Sugar, No Fat Cookbook
Quick and Easy Pasta Recipes
Cooking in Clay
Deep Fried Indulgences
The Garlic Cookbook
From Your Ice Cream Maker
The Best Pizza is Made at Home
The Best Bagels are Made at Home
Convection Oven Cookery
The Steamer Cookbook
The Pasta Machine Cookbook
The Versatile Rice Cooker
The Bread Machine Cookbook
The Bread Machine Cookbook II
The Bread Machine Cookbook III
The Bread Machine Cookbook IV:
  Whole Grains & Natural Sugars
The Bread Machine Cookbook V:
  *Favorite Recipes from 100
  Kitchens*

The Bread Machine Cookbook VI:
  *Hand-Shaped Breads from the
  Dough Cycle*
Worldwide Sourdoughs from Your
  Bread Machine
Entrées from Your Bread Machine
The New Blender Book
The Sandwich Maker Cookbook
Waffles
The Coffee Book
The Juicer Book I and II
Bread Baking
The 9 x 13 Pan Cookbook
Recipes for the Loaf Pan
Low Fat American Favorites
Healthy Cooking on the Run
Favorite Seafood Recipes
New International Fondue Cookbook
Favorite Cookie Recipes
Cooking for 1 or 2
The Well Dressed Potato
Extra-Special Crockery Pot Recipes
Slow Cooking
The Wok

**For a free catalog, write or call: Bristol Publishing Enterprises, Inc.
P.O. Box 1737, San Leandro, CA 94577 (800) 346-4889**